Quick QUILTS with Rulers

PAM &
NICKY
LINTOTT

18
easy quilt
patterns

D&C
David and Charles

www.stitchcraftcreate.co.uk

This content has been previously published in the following booklets by Lynher Publications

Three Patterns Featuring Creative Grids® Double-strip Kaleidoscope Ruler
Three Patterns Featuring Creative Grids® Multi-Size 2 Peaks in 1 Triangle Ruler
Flying Geese Multi-Size

Contents

Introduction

We know that quilters love gadgets and rulers are the ultimate gadgets for quilters. Somewhere we all have clever rulers tucked away which we have bought as they looked so quick and easy to use. We also know that many of those rulers are not used very often, but what a waste. Rulers really do make cutting and creating easier – it is just important that we know how to use them.

In this book we have chosen three rulers that certainly make life easier and although we have used the Creative Grids brand of rulers there are many other brands on the market which do the same job. So we beg you to search through your cupboards and dig out rulers you haven't used for a while and the chances are you will find rulers which do the same job. If not, then you might think about treating yourself to one – rulers really are worth their weight in gold.

Now don't think for a moment we have fallen out of love with jelly rolls. Our jelly roll quilt books have sold over 350,000 copies worldwide and we love the strip method of quiltmaking. All the quilts in this book start with strips – although strips of many different widths. You will also see that a number of jelly roll quilts have popped into this book as well – how did that happen!

Our first ruler is the Creative Grids Two Peaks in One ruler. Now this ruler might be called by a different name so do have a thorough search for it in your cupboards. This ruler makes the clever unit found in the Storm at Sea pattern and it was also called Peaky & Spike by the late Doreen Speckmann. The Tri-Recs ruler can also be used. It is important to remember that when using different rulers you need to make sure you are cutting on the correct markings.

Our second choice of ruler is the Creative Grids Double Strip Kaleidoscope ruler. There are lots of kaleidoscope rulers and any one of them will make the quilts in this book. This really is a great one to impress family and friends with your speed and creativity. Our Friday Night quilt really was made on a Friday night, making it a great one to choose if you need a quilt in a hurry. It is also a perfect choice for a beginner. Our Two to Tango quilt shows the different effect created when you use jelly roll strips.

Our third ruler is the Creative Grids Multi-Size Flying Geese ruler. We love the simplicity and versatility of this ruler. It has a 90 degree triangle that is used to make the centre of the flying geese unit on one side of the ruler and a 45 degree triangle that is used to make the side triangles on the other side. This means that as well as having a flying geese ruler, you also have a 45 degree triangle that is perfect for making half-square triangles from strips, and a large 90 degree triangle that can be used for strip-tube cutting and lots more. Check out our Geometric Breeze quilt to see how to use it for strip-tube cutting.

So have we inspired you to go searching for those rulers? We hope so and we hope you like making the quilts in this book.

Getting Started

Tools

All the projects in this book require rotary cutting equipment. You will need a self-healing cutting mat at least 18in x 24in and a rotary cutter. We recommend the 45mm or the 60mm diameter rotary cutter. Any rotary cutting work requires rulers and most people have a make they prefer. We like the Creative Grids rulers as their markings are clear, they do not slip on fabric and their Turn-a-Round facility is so useful when dealing with half-inch measurements. We recommend the 6½in x 24in as a basic ruler plus a large square no less than 12½in, which is handy for squaring up and making sure you are always cutting at right angles.

Seams

We cannot stress enough the importance of maintaining an accurate ¼in seam allowance throughout. We prefer to say an accurate *scant* ¼in seam because there are two factors to take into account. Firstly, the thickness of thread and secondly, when the seam allowance is pressed to one side it takes up a tiny amount of fabric. These are both extremely small amounts but if they are ignored you will find your *exact* ¼in seam allowance is taking up more than ¼in. So, it is well worth testing your seam allowance before starting on a quilt and most sewing machines have various needle positions that can be used to make any adjustments.

Seam allowance test

Take a 2½in strip and cut off three segments each 1½in wide. Sew two segments together down the longer side and press the seam to one side. Sew the third segment across the top. It should fit exactly. If it doesn't, you need to make an adjustment to your seam allowance. If it is too long, your seam allowance is too wide and can be corrected by moving the needle on your sewing machine to the right. If it is too small, your seam allowance is too narrow and this can be corrected by moving the needle to the left.

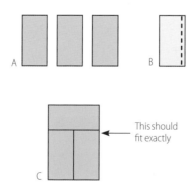

This should fit exactly

Imperial or Metric?

The specialist rulers we have used are all marked in inches, therefore all our instructions are written in inches. To convert inches to centimetres, multiply the inch measurement by 2.54. For your convenience, any extra fabric you will need, given in the Requirements panel at the start of the quilt instructions, is given in both metric and imperial.

Quilt and Fabric Sizes

The size of each of the quilts in this book is given in the Vital Statistics information at the beginning of the project instructions but you could, of course, use more fabric and increase the size of your quilt.

All of our patterns are based on fabric being 42in wide. If our requirements use half yards then we assume that you have 42in x 17½in of usable fabric. If we use fat quarters we assume you have 21in x 17½in. This allows a little leeway for straightening up your strips, but not a lot, so take care not to be wasteful when trimming selvedges. If you are working in half and quarter metres rather than yards then you will have a little extra fabric to work with.

Diagrams

Diagrams are provided to help you make the quilts, normally beneath or beside the relevant stepped instruction. The direction in which fabric should be pressed is indicated by arrows on the diagrams. The reverse side of the fabric is shown in a lighter colour than the right side.

Alternative Templates

The quilts in the book can also be made with templates, which we have supplied at the end of the book. These aren't as versatile as the specialist rulers but will allow you to make the quilts in this book.

Before You Start

Before you dive into making a quilt please read the instructions fully and don't forget to keep that scant ¼in seam allowance. Most of all – have fun. We designed these quilts to be easy to make and we hope they will be well used and loved. The techniques we use do encourage accuracy but no one is going to be judging you on every last point!

2 PEAKS IN 1

MULTI-SIZE NON-SLIP TRIANGLE RULER

The Multi-Size Non-Slip 2 Peaks in 1 Triangle Ruler is an innovative ruler by Rachel Cross of Creative Grids®. The unique concept that sets this all-in-one ruler apart is that just by rotating it you can create many well-loved block units quickly and easily with minimum fuss and fabric wastage.

In the following section of the book we show you great ways to use this ruler. Not only will you get to make great quilts quickly and easily – great for a weekend project – but it will also leave you feeling inspired and wanting to make more of your own unique creations!

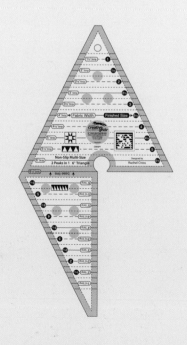

Flower Power

We wanted this quilt to really sparkle and the gorgeously bright Kaffe Fassett prints certainly do that, especially when teamed with a pale background. This is a great quilt to get you started on using the Multi-Size 2 Peaks in 1 Triangle ruler as it's just thirty-five repeated blocks with a simple narrow border. But be warned, once you start using this ruler you will get hooked!

Vital Statistics

Quilt size:	49in x 67in
Block size:	9in
Number of blocks:	35
Setting:	5 x 7 blocks, plus 2in wide border

Requirements

- Four assorted ½yd/m of fabric for the flowers
- Four assorted ½yd/m of fabric for the background
- ½yd/m of fabric for the border
- Fabric for binding is included in the ½yd/m

Cutting Instructions

FLOWER FABRIC

1 Cut each of the four assorted ½yds for the flowers as follows.

- Three 5in wide strips cut across the width of the fabric. These will be used to make your flowers. You will have twelve 5in flower strips. Keep these folded.
- One 2½in wide strip cut across the width of the fabric. Set the four 2½in strips aside for the scrappy binding.

2 Working with one 5in flower strip at a time and keeping it folded, place the centre triangle of the Multi-Size 2 Peaks in 1 Triangle as far to the left of the strip as possible. Don't start at the fold end as your excess fabric will be needed for the appliqué flower centres and it is more useful for this to be in one piece.

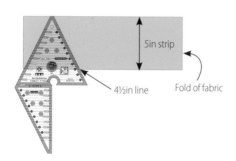

- Align the *4½in marked line (5in strip width)* of the centre triangle with the bottom of the strip and the cut-off top of the triangle with the top of the strip. Cut your first triangle – this is the first 'petal'.

3 Rotate the triangle 180 degrees and cut the second triangle. Continue to cut six pairs of triangles making a total of twelve triangles. This will make three flowers using four petals for each. Don't discard excess fabric as this is needed to make the appliqué flower centres.

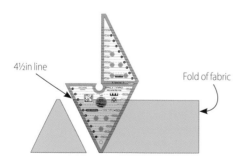

4 Repeat with all twelve 5in flower strips to make a total of 144 triangles – thirty-six from each ½yd. You need 140 so four are spare.

BACKGROUND FABRIC

5 Take each of the four ½yds of background fabric and subcut them as follows.

- Three 5in wide strips cut across the width of the fabric. Keep these strips folded for cutting. You will have twelve 5in background strips.
- One 2½in wide strip cut across the width of the fabric. Set two aside for the binding. The remaining two 2½in wide strips are spare.

6 Take one 5in background strip and *keeping it folded*, trim the selvedge and lay the side triangle of the Multi-Size 2 Peaks in 1 Triangle on the strip as shown, aligning the *4½in marked line (5in strip width)* with the bottom of the strip and the cut-off top of the triangle with the top of the strip. Cut one triangle. Note: *Keeping the strip folded is very important when cutting this shape as you need a pair of reverse triangles.*

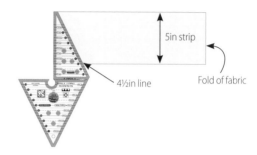

7 Rotate the triangle 180 degrees and cut the second triangle. Continue to make twelve pairs of triangles. You will have twelve triangles and twelve reverse triangles.

- Repeat with all twelve 5in background strips to make a total of 144 pairs of side triangles – half of these will be reverse triangles. You need 140 triangles and 140 reverse triangles in total, so four pairs are spare.

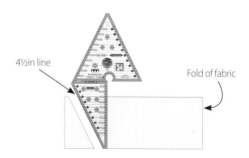

BORDER FABRIC

8 Cut six 2½in wide strips across the width of the fabric.

Making the Blocks

1 Choose four petals of the same fabric and four left-hand side triangles and four right-hand side triangles of the same fabric.

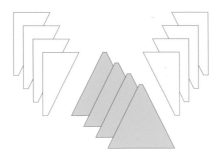

2 Sew a right-hand side triangle to the right-hand side of a petal triangle. You will notice that the pieces will appear ¼in out at each end but this is because you have an angled cut. It is important that your pieces are aligned at the top and bottom after sewing so double check before you sew. Press towards the background fabric.

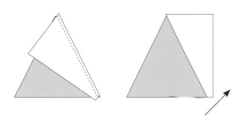

TIP

Fold both the centre triangle and the side triangle to find the centres of the edges to be sewn. Mark each with a pin and these can then be matched up before sewing to ensure that you are positioning the triangles in the correct places.

3 Sew a left-hand side triangle to the unit and press to the background fabric. Repeat with three other petal triangles of the same fabric.

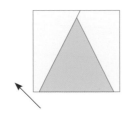

4 Each petal unit should measure 5in square so check each unit and trim to size if necessary. If your units are measuring under 5in then reduce your seam allowance slightly.

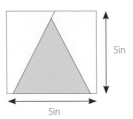

5 Rotate the four petal units as shown and sew the top two together pressing the seams to the right. Sew the bottom two together and press the seams to the left. Then sew the pairs together and press. Pin at every seam intersection to ensure a perfect match. Your first flower block has been made. Repeat to make thirty-five flower blocks.

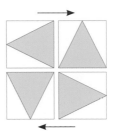

Making the Flower Centres

6 The excess fabric from the 5in flower strips is used to make the flower centres. You need to make three flower centres from the excess fabric from each strip

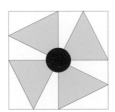

7 Draw a 1½in diameter circle on thin card and cut it out to use as a template. Using the card circle as a guide, cut out fabric circles approximately ¼in larger all the way round. Place the card circle on the wrong side of the fabric circle and sew a running stitch around the outside of the card circle. Pull the stitches up tightly around the cardboard circle and knot to hold in place.

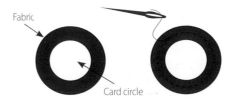

Fabric

Card circle

Sew around the edge and pull tight around the card

8 Press the edge firmly with an iron to crease all round and then carefully remove the cardboard circle. Pin the flower centre right side up in the centre of one of the flowers and appliqué in place with matching thread and small slip stitches. Repeat with all thirty-five flowers.

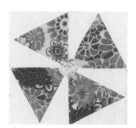

Assembling the Quilt

9 Lay out your flower blocks into seven rows of five blocks and when you are happy with the layout sew the blocks into rows and then sew the rows together. Press the seams in row one to the left and the seams in row two to the right, so your seams will nest together nicely when sewing the rows together.

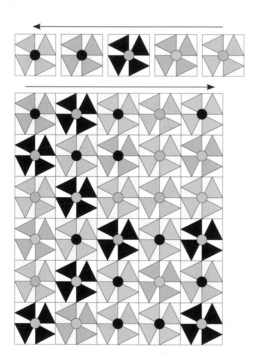

Adding the Border

10 Join the six border strips into a continuous length. Determine the vertical measurement from top to bottom through the centre of your quilt top. Cut two side borders to this measurement.

11 Mark the halves and quarters of one quilt side and one border with pins. Placing right sides together and matching the pins, stitch quilt and border together, easing the quilt side to fit where necessary. Repeat on the opposite side. Press the seams.

12 Determine the horizontal measurement from side to side across the centre of the quilt top. Cut two borders to this measurement. Pin and sew to the top and bottom of your quilt and press.

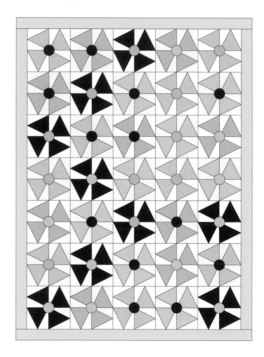

13 Your quilt is now finished. Quilt as desired and bind to finish.

14 If you wish to make a scrappy binding, cut the 2½in strips set aside for the binding into 2½in x 10½in rectangles. Sew together to make a continuous strip, alternating the colours. You need about 250in. Note: If you are working with metres, which give a little extra fabric, you can substitute the background strips for strips cut from your spare flower fabric if you prefer.

TIP
Pins are your best friends! Pinning at every seam intersection will ensure your seams match perfectly. When sewing do not remove the pin too early as your fabric might shift and your seams will not be perfectly aligned.

We used gorgeous Kaffe Fassett fabrics to create this bright and cheerful quilt, which also has a great sense of movement. For a speedier quilt the appliqué flower centres could be omitted and a totally different effect would be created. This quilt was made by the authors and longarm quilted by The Quilt Room.

Roman Holiday

The pretty colours of this striking quilt sing out to us and we can just imagine sipping a cool drink in the hot Italian sunshine under a bright blue sky – a Gregory Peck look-alike would be an added bonus – sorry, we're getting carried away! You are all probably far too young to remember the film of this name but you're sure to enjoy making this lovely quilt!

Vital Statistics

Quilt Size:	68in x 68in
Block Size:	12in
Number of Blocks:	16 Flower blocks and 9 Snowball blocks
Setting:	On point

• •

Requirements

- ¾yd (60cm) of aqua fabric
- 2yd (1.75m) of cream fabric
- 1½yd (1.25m) of pink fabric (or for variety three different pinks ½yd/m of each)
- 20in (50cm) of red fabric
- 20in (50cm) each of green and blue fabric for setting triangles
- ½yd/m of binding fabric

Cutting Instructions

AQUA FABRIC

1 Cut five 4½in wide strips across the width of the fabric.

- Take one of the five 4½in wide strips, open it out and place the centre triangle of the Multi-Size 2 Peaks in 1 Triangle as far to the left of the strip as possible. Align the *4in marked line* (4½in strip width) on the triangle with the bottom of the strip and the cut-off top of the triangle with the top of the strip. Cut your first triangle.
- Repeat with all five 4½in aqua strips to make a total of sixty-five triangles. You need sixty-four so one will be spare.

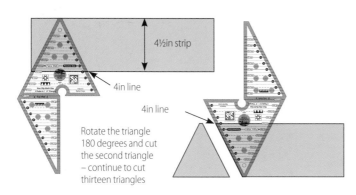

4½in strip

4in line

4in line

Rotate the triangle 180 degrees and cut the second triangle – continue to cut thirteen triangles

CREAM FABRIC

2 Cut thirteen 4½in wide strips across the width of the fabric.

- Take eight of the 4½in wide strips and subcut each strip into eight 4½in squares to make a total of sixty-four 4½in squares.
- Cut the remaining five strips as follows:

  - Cutting one strip at a time and *keeping it folded*, trim the selvedge and lay the side triangle of the Multi-Size 2 Peaks in 1 Triangle on the strip as shown. Align the *4in line* with the bottom of the strip and the cut-off top of the triangle with the top of the strip. Cut one triangle.

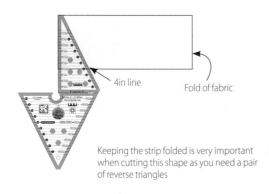

4in line

Fold of fabric

Keeping the strip folded is very important when cutting this shape as you need a pair of reverse triangles

- Rotate the triangle 180 degrees and cut the second triangle. Continue like this to cut thirteen pairs of triangles and thirteen reverse triangles.

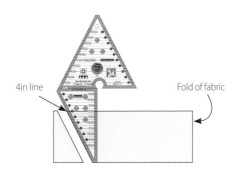

4in line

Fold of fabric

- Repeat with all five 4½in cream strips to make a total of sixty-five pairs of side triangles – half of these will be reverse triangles. You need sixty-four pairs in total so one pair is spare.

PINK FABRIC

3 Cut three 12½in wide strips across the width of the fabric. Subcut each of the three strips into three 12½in squares to make a total of nine 12½in squares.

- With the remaining pink fabric, cut two 4½in strips across the width of the fabric and subcut each strip into eight 4½in squares. You need sixteen in total for the flower block centres.

RED FABRIC

4 Cut four 4½in strips across the width of the fabric and subcut each strip into nine 4½in squares. You need thirty-six for the snowball corners.

SETTING AND CORNER TRIANGLES

5 Cut one green strip 18½in wide across the width of the fabric and subcut into two 18½in squares. Cut across both diagonals of the two 18½in squares to form eight green setting triangles.

- Cut one blue strip 18½in wide across the width of the fabric and subcut into one 18½in square. Cut across both diagonals of the 18½in square to form four blue setting triangles.

- Using the excess from the 18½in blue strip, trim to measure 10in wide and cut two 10in squares. Cut across one diagonal of each square to form four corner triangles. Cutting the setting and corner triangles this way ensures the outer edges of your quilt are not on the bias.

BINDING FABRIC

6 Cut seven 2½in wide strips across the width of the fabric.

Making the Flower Blocks

1 Take an aqua triangle and a pair of cream side triangles. Sew the right-hand cream triangle to the right side of an aqua triangle. You will notice that the pieces will appear ¼in out at each end but this is because you have an angled cut. It is important that your pieces are aligned at the top and bottom once sewn, so double check before sewing. Press towards the background fabric.

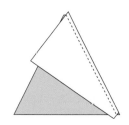 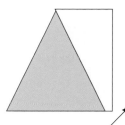

TIP

Fold both the centre triangle and the side triangle to find the centres of the edges to be sewn. Mark each with a pin and these can then be matched up before sewing to ensure that you are positioning the triangles in the correct places.

2 Sew a left-hand cream triangle to the unit. Press towards the background fabric.

3 Repeat with all sixty-four aqua triangles. Each 2 peaks in 1 triangle unit should measure 4½in square so check each unit and trim to size if necessary. If your units are measuring under 4½in then reduce your seam allowance slightly.

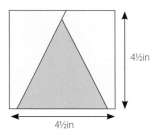

4½in

4½in

4 Sew two 4½in cream squares to each side of the 2 peaks in 1 triangle unit. Press towards the squares. Repeat to make thirty-two units.

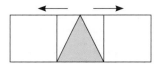

5 Sew two 2 peaks in 1 triangle units to each side of a 4½in pink square. Press towards the pink square. Repeat to make sixteen units.

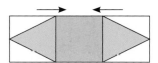

6 Sew these units together as shown, pinning at every seam intersection to ensure a perfect match and press as shown. Repeat to make sixteen Flower blocks.

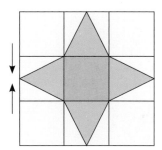

Making the Snowball Blocks

7 Mark a diagonal line from corner to corner on the wrong side of four of the 4½in square red snowball corners.

8 With right sides together, lay a marked square on one corner of a 12½in pink square, aligning the outer edges. Sew across the diagonal, using the marked diagonal line as the stitching line. An alternative is to fold the square and use the fold to guide you.

9 Flip the square over and press towards the outside of the block. Trim the excess fabric from the red snowball corner but do not trim the pink fabric. Although this creates a little more bulk, the pink square helps keep your patchwork in shape. Repeat on the other three corners.

10 Repeat this process to make nine Snowball blocks.

Setting the Blocks on Point

11 Referring to the quilt diagram, lay out the blocks as shown. When you are happy with the layout, sew a green setting triangle to each side of a Flower block to create row one. The setting triangles have been cut slightly larger to make the blocks 'float', so when sewing the setting triangles make sure the bottom of the triangle is aligned with the block. Press as shown in the diagram.

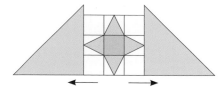

12 Sew row two together with blue setting triangles at both ends.

13 Continue to sew the blocks together to form rows with alternate coloured setting triangles at each end. Always press away from the Flower blocks as this will ensure your seams are going in different directions when sewing the rows together.

14 Sew the rows together, pinning at every intersection. Sew the blue corner triangles on last.

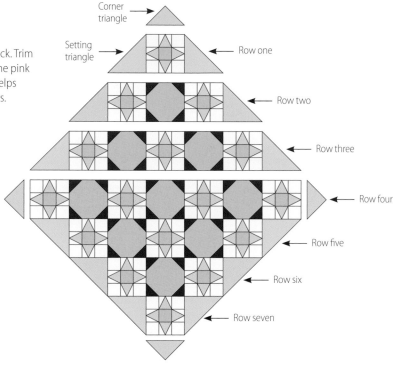

15 Your quilt is now complete. Quilt as desired and bind to finish.

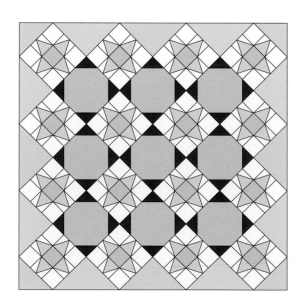

Vibrant fabrics for a stunning looking quilt – bright aqua, pink, green and red – wow, we love it! These fabrics are from the Flower Sugar collection from Lecien. Attractively set on point and alternating with the ever-useful Snowball block, this is a quick quilt to make. This quilt was made by the authors and longarm quilted by The Quilt Room.

Stargazing

We love the contrasting fabrics that allow this curvy design to really shine. The illusion of curves is created by combining the Fifty-Four Forty or Fight block with the oh-so-useful Snowball block. We were aiming for a quilt that wasn't too 'girly', with a bit more boyish charm. The open spaces lend themselves to some great quilting. Our quilt was longarm quilted but some hand-quilted motifs in these open spaces would also be perfect.

Vital Statistics

Quilt Size:	70in x 70in
Block Size:	12in
Number of Blocks:	13 Fifty-four Forty or Fight blocks and 12 Snowball blocks
Setting:	5 x 5 blocks, plus 1in inner border and 4in outer border

Requirements

- Five fat quarters from different fabrics – tan and black for the centre blocks and pink, aqua and blue for the four-patch blocks
- 1¼yd (1.10m) of red fabric
- 20in (50cm) of light grey fabric
- 1½yd (1.40m) of light neutral fabric for large squares
- 1yd (75cm) of brown fabric for snowball corners
- 1yd (1m) of fabric for outer border
- ½yd (50cm) of binding fabric

Cutting Instructions

TAN AND BLACK FAT QUARTERS

1 Making sure you are cutting down the 21in length, cut four 2⅞in wide strips from each of the two fat quarters. These 2⅞in x 21in strips will be used for making the centre half-square triangle units.

PINK, BLUE AND AQUA FAT QUARTERS

2 Making sure you are cutting down the 21in length, cut seven 2½in strips from each of the three fat quarters. They will measure 2½in x 21in.

RED FABRIC

3 Cut four 4½in wide strips across the width of the fabric. These are for the side triangles of the 2 peaks in 1 triangle unit.

- Cut four 2½in wide strips across the width of the fabric and subcut each into two rectangles 2½in x 21in. Seven will be used in the four-patch blocks and one rectangle is spare.
- Cut seven 1½in wide strips across the width of the fabric and set aside for the inner border.

LIGHT GREY FABRIC

4 Cut four 4½in wide strips across the width of the fabric. These are for the centre triangles of the 2 peaks in 1 triangle unit.

LIGHT NEUTRAL FABRIC

5 Cut four 12½in wide strips and subcut each into three 12½in wide squares to make a total of twelve 12½in squares.

BROWN FABRIC

6 Cut six 4½in wide strips across the width of the fabric. Subcut each strip into eight 4½in squares. You need forty-eight in total for the snowball corners.

OUTER BORDER FABRIC

7 Cut seven 4½in wide strips across the width of the fabric.

BINDING FABRIC

8 Cut seven 2½in wide strips across the width of the fabric.

Making the Centre Units

1 Take one tan 2⅞in x 21in strip and one black 2⅞in x 21in strip and press right sides together.

2 Lay the paired strips on a cutting mat and cut into seven 2⅞in squares. Repeat with all four pairs of tan and black strips to make a total of twenty-eight pairs of squares.

3 Cut each pair of squares diagonally through the centre to make fifty-six pairs of triangles. Keeping the triangles together, sew down the diagonal of each pair, chain piecing for speed. Trim the dog ears.

4 Open the units and press half towards the black fabric and press the other half towards the tan fabric.

Make 28   Make 28

5 Take two units pressed in different directions and with right sides together sew them as shown. Press to the left. Repeat to make twenty-six of these units. Four units are spare.

6 Take two of these units and rotate one 180 degrees. Sew together as shown in the diagram to make thirteen centre units. Press the seams.

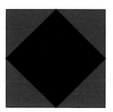

Making the 2 Peaks in 1 Triangle Units

7 Take one 4½in light grey strip and lay the centre triangle of the Multi-Size 2 Peaks in 1 Triangle on the strip as far to the left as possible. Align the *4in line (4½in strip width)* with the bottom of the strip and the cut-off top of the triangle with the top of the strip. Cut one triangle. Rotate the triangle 180 degrees and cut the second triangle. Continue to the end of the strip, rotating the ruler, to make thirteen triangles.

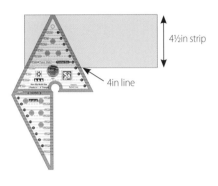

4in line

8 Repeat with all four 4½in light grey strips to make fifty-two triangles.

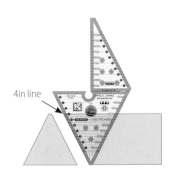

4in line

9 Take one 4½in red strip and *keeping it folded*, trim the selvedge. Lay the side triangle of the Multi-Size 2 Peaks in 1 Triangle on the strip as shown, aligning the *4in line* with the bottom of the strip and the cut-off top of the triangle with the top of the strip. Cut one triangle. Note: *Keeping the strip folded is very important when cutting this shape as you need a pair of reverse triangles.*

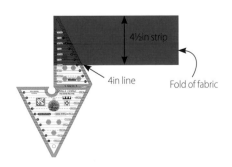

4½in strip

4in line

Fold of fabric

10 Rotate the triangle 180 degrees and cut the second triangle. Continue to the end of the strip to make thirteen pairs of side triangles – thirteen triangles and thirteen reverse triangles. Repeat with all four 4½in red strips to make a total of fifty-two side triangles and fifty-two reverse side triangles.

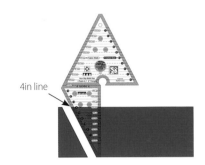

4in line

11 Take a light grey centre triangle and a pair of red side triangles. Sew the right side triangle to the right side of a centre triangle. You will notice that the pieces will appear ¼in out at each end but this is because you have an angled cut. It is important that your pieces are aligned at the top and bottom once sewn, so double check before sewing. Press away from the centre triangle.

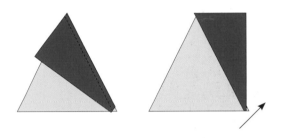

> **TIP**
>
> Fold both the centre triangle and the side triangle to find the centres of the edges to be sewn. Mark each with a pin and these can then be matched up before sewing to ensure that you are positioning the triangles in the correct places.

12 Sew a left red triangle to the unit and press away from the centre triangle. The unit should measure 4½in square. If your units are measuring under 4½in then reduce your seam allowance slightly. Repeat to make fifty-two 2 peaks in 1 triangle units.

Making the Four-Patch Units

13 Take a red and a blue 2½in x 21in strip and with right sides together sew down the long side. Open and press towards the blue fabric. Repeat with all seven red and blue 2½in x 21in strips.

14 Take an aqua and a pink 2½in x 21in strip and with right sides together sew down the long side. Open and press to the aqua fabric. Repeat with all seven aqua and pink 2½in x 21in strips.

15 With right sides together, lay a red and blue strip unit on top of an aqua and pink strip unit, ensuring that the centre seams are in alignment. Make sure the fabrics are positioned as shown in the diagram and be consistent with all strip units.

16 Cut the strip unit into eight 2½in wide segments. Repeat with all seven pairs of strip units to make a total of fifty-six pairs of segments. You need fifty-two so you will have four spare.

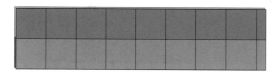

17 Carefully keeping the pairs together, sew down the long side as shown on twenty-six of the pairs. Pin at the seam intersection to ensure a perfect match. The seams will nest together nicely as they are pressed in different directions. Chain piece for speed. Press open to form twenty-six four-patch (A) units as shown.

Unit A – make 26

18 Rotate the remaining twenty-six pairs 180 degrees and sew down the long side as shown. Press open to form twenty-six four-patch (B) units as shown.

Unit B – make 26

Assembling the Fifty-Four Forty or Fight Blocks

19 Take a 2 peaks in 1 triangle unit and sew a four-patch unit A to the right side and a four-patch unit B to the left side, making sure the red squares are placed as shown in the diagram. Make two of these rows. Press towards the four-patch blocks.

20 Sew a 2 peaks in 1 triangle unit to either side of a centre square unit. Press towards the centre.

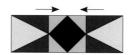

21 Sew the rows together, pinning at every seam intersection to ensure a perfect match. Press seams away from the centre. Repeat to make thirteen blocks.

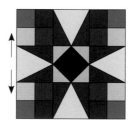

Making the Snowball Blocks

22 Draw a diagonal line from corner to corner on the wrong side of four 4½in squares allocated for the snowball block corners.

23 With right sides together, lay a marked square on one corner of a 12½in light neutral square, aligning the outer edges. Sew across the diagonal, using the marked diagonal line as the stitching line. Alternatively, mark the line with a fold to help stitch this line accurately.

24 Flip the square over and press towards the outside of the block. Trim the excess fabric from the snowball corner but do not trim the light fabric. Although this creates a little more bulk, the light fabric helps keep your patchwork in shape. Repeat on all four corners. Repeat to make twelve Snowball blocks.

 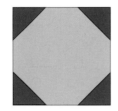

Assembling the Quilt

25 Layout your blocks into five rows of five blocks alternating the blocks as shown in the diagram. Sew the blocks into rows, pinning at every seam intersection and then sew the rows together. Press the seams towards the Snowball blocks so your seams will nest together nicely when the rows are sewn together.

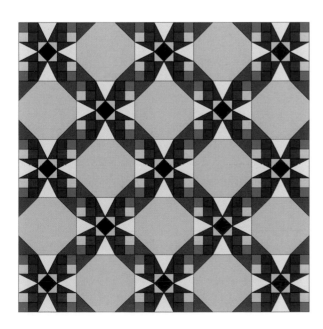

Adding the Borders

26 Sew the seven 1½in wide strips for the inner border into a continuous length. Measure the quilt through the centre from top to bottom. Cut two side borders to this measurement. Pin mark the halves and quarters of one quilt side and one border. Placing right sides together and matching the pins, stitch quilt and border together, easing the quilt side to fit. Repeat on the opposite side and then press. Now measure the quilt through the centre from side to side. Cut two borders to this measurement. Pin and sew to the top and bottom of your quilt and press.

27 Repeat this process to add the outer border, using the seven 4½in strips.

28 Your quilt top is now complete. Quilt as desired and bind to finish.

Don't you just love it when straight sewing creates curves! We used a selection of Japanese taupes including some lovely woven fabrics, which added extra texture. This quilt was made by the authors and longarm quilted by The Quilt Room.

Starry Skies

When designing our quilts we always play around with various alternating blocks. This quilt is a variation of the Stargazing quilt but it works so well with the Shoo Fly block that we couldn't resist making it. We have also used more variety of fabric in this quilt, which gives the quilt a scrappier, softer look.

Vital Statistics

Quilt Size:	70in x 70in
Block Size:	12in
Number of Blocks:	13 Fifty-Four Forty or Fight blocks and 12 Shoo Fly blocks
Setting:	5 x 5 blocks, plus 1in border and 4in outer border

Requirements

- Three fat quarters of different fabrics for the four-patch blocks – aqua, coffee and green
- Four ½yd/m of fabric – two yellow and two blue for both block centres and the corner 4in half-square triangle units in the Shoo Fly blocks
- Three ½yd/m of apricot fabric
- Four ½yd/m of light fabric for the 4in squares in the Shoo Fly blocks and the centre triangles of the 2 peaks in 1 triangle units
- 1yd (1m) of fabric for outer border
- ½yd (50cm) of binding fabric

Cutting Instructions

AQUA, COFFEE AND GREEN FAT QUARTERS

1 Making sure you are cutting down the 21in length, cut seven 2½in strips from each of the three fat quarters. Each strip will then measure 2½in x 21in.

YELLOW AND BLUE FABRICS

2 Cut the yellow fabric as follows:

- Take one yellow ½yd and cut four 2⅞in wide strips across the width of the fabric. These will be used to make the centre 2in finished half-square triangle units in both blocks.
- With the remaining yellow ½yd, cut three 4⅞in wide strips across the width of the fabric. These will be used to make the 4in *finished* half-square triangle units in the Shoo Fly blocks.
- Repeat this cutting with the blue fabrics.

APRICOT FABRIC

3 Cut four 4½in wide strips across the width of the fabric. These are for the side triangles of the 2 peaks in 1 triangle units.

- Cut four 2½in wide strips across the width of the fabric and subcut each into two rectangles 2½in x 21in. Seven will be used in the four-patch blocks and one rectangle is spare.
- Cut seven 1½in wide strips across the width of the fabric and set aside for the inner border.

LIGHT FABRIC

4 Cut ten 4½in wide strips across the width of the fabric.

- Subcut six of these strips into eight 4½in squares each, to make forty-eight 4½in squares for the Shoo Fly blocks.
- Leave four strips uncut for the centre triangles of the 2 peaks in 1 triangle units.

OUTER BORDER FABRIC

5 Cut seven 4½in wide strips across the width of the fabric.

BINDING FABRIC

6 Cut seven 2½in wide strips across the width of the fabric.

Making the Centre Units

1 The centre squares for both the Fifty-Four Forty or Fight block and the Shoo Fly block are made up of half-square triangle units, are made in the same way and can be made at the same time. Take one yellow 2⅞in x 42in strip and one blue 2⅞in x 42in strip and press right sides together.

2 Lay the paired strips on a cutting mat and cut into thirteen 2⅞in squares. Repeat with all four pairs of yellow and blue 2⅞in strips to make a total of fifty two pairs of squares.

3 Cut each pair of 2⅞in squares diagonally through the centre to make 104 pairs of triangles. Keeping the triangles together, sew down the diagonal of each pair, chain piecing for speed. Trim the dog ears.

4 Open and press half towards the yellow fabric and the other half towards the blue fabric. These will measure 2½in square (finished 2in half-square triangle unit).

Make 28   Make 28

5 Take two units pressed in different directions and with right sides together sew them together as shown. Press to the left. Repeat to make fifty-two of these units. Only fifty are needed, so two units are spare.

6 Take two of these units and rotate one 180 degrees. Sew together as shown in the diagram to make twenty-five centre units. Press the seams. Thirteen centres are for the Fifty-Four Forty or Fight blocks and twelve centres are for the Shoo Fly blocks.

Making the Shoo Fly Blocks

7 Using the three pairs of yellow and blue 4⅞in x 42in strips, cut eight 4⅞in squares from each pair of strips. Using the same technique as in steps 3–5 (making 2in half-square triangle units), make forty-eight half-square triangle units. These will measure 4½in square (finished 4in half-square triangle unit). These are for the corners of the block.

8 Assemble the block by following the layout in the diagram below, positioning a centre unit and the light 4½in squares with the 4in *finished* half-square triangle units in the four corners. Sew the units together in rows and then sew the rows together. Repeat to make twelve Shoo Fly blocks.

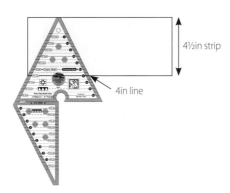

Making the 2 Peaks in 1 Triangle Units

9 Take one 4½in light strip and lay the centre triangle of the Multi-Size 2 Peaks in 1 Triangle on the strip as far to the left as possible. Align the *4in line* (4½in strip width) with the bottom of the strip and the cut-off top of the triangle with the top of the strip. Cut one triangle.

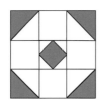

10 Rotate the triangle 180 degrees and cut the second triangle. Continue to the end of the strip, rotating the ruler, to cut thirteen triangles. Repeat with all four 4½in light strips to make a total of fifty-two triangles.

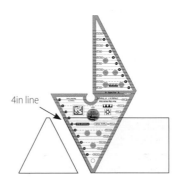

11 Take one 4½in apricot strip and *keeping it folded*, trim the selvedge. Lay the side triangle of the Multi-Size 2 Peaks in 1 Triangle on the strip as shown, aligning the *4in line* with the bottom of the strip and the cut-off top of the triangle with the top of the strip. Cut one triangle. Note: *Keeping the strip folded is very important when cutting this shape as you need a pair of reverse triangles.*

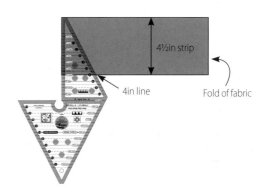

12 Rotate the triangle 180 degrees and cut the second triangle. Continue to the end of the strip to make thirteen pairs of side triangles – thirteen triangles and thirteen reverse triangles. Repeat with all four 4½in apricot strips to make a total of fifty-two side triangles and fifty-two reverse side triangles.

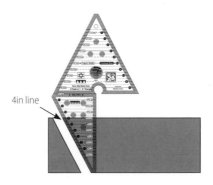

13 Take a light centre triangle and a pair of apricot side triangles. Sew the right side triangle to the right side of a centre triangle. You will notice that the pieces will appear ¼in out at each end but this is because you have an angled cut. It is important that your pieces are aligned at the top and bottom once sewn, so double check before sewing. Press away from the centre triangle.

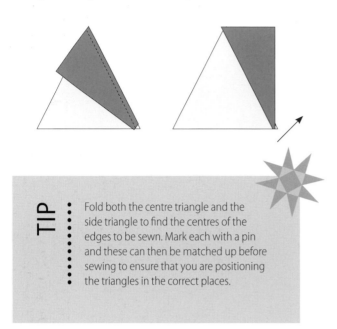

TIP Fold both the centre triangle and the side triangle to find the centres of the edges to be sewn. Mark each with a pin and these can then be matched up before sewing to ensure that you are positioning the triangles in the correct places.

14 Sew a left apricot triangle to the unit and press away from the centre triangle. The unit should measure 4½in square. If your units are measuring under 4½in then reduce your seam allowance slightly. Repeat to make fifty-two 2 peaks in 1 triangle units.

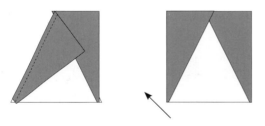

Making the Four-Patch Units

15 Take an apricot and an aqua 2½in x 21in strip and with right sides together sew down the long side. Open and press towards the aqua fabric. Repeat with all seven apricot and aqua 2½in x 21in strips.

16 Take a green and a coffee 2½in x 21in strip and with right sides together sew down the long side. Open and press to the green fabric. Repeat with all seven green and coffee 2½in x 21in strips.

17 With right sides together, lay an apricot and aqua strip unit on top of a green and coffee strip unit, ensuring that the centre seams are in alignment. Make sure the fabrics are positioned as shown in the diagram and be consistent with all strip units.

18 Cut the strip unit into eight 2½in wide segments. Repeat with all seven pairs of strip units to make a total of fifty-six pairs of segments. You need fifty-two so you will have four spare.

19 Carefully keeping the pairs together, sew down the long side on twenty-six of the pairs. Pin at the seam intersection to ensure a perfect match. The seams will nest together nicely as they are pressed in different directions. Chain piece for speed. Press open to form twenty-six four-patch (A) units as shown.

Unit A – make 26

20 Rotate the remaining twenty-six pairs 180 degrees and sew down the long side. Press open to form twenty-six four-patch (B) units.

Unit B – make 26

Assembling the Fifty-Four Forty or Fight Blocks

21 Take a 2 Peaks in 1 triangle unit and sew a four-patch unit A to the right side and a four-patch unit B to the left side, making sure the apricot squares are placed as shown in the diagram. Make two of these rows. Press towards the four-patch blocks.

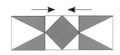

22 Sew a 2 Peaks in 1 triangle unit to either side of a centre square unit. Press towards the centre.

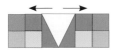

23 Sew the rows together, pinning at every seam intersection to ensure a perfect match. Press seams away from the centre. Repeat to make thirteen blocks.

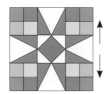

Assembling the Quilt

24 Lay out your blocks as shown, alternating the two blocks. Arrange into five rows of five blocks. When you are happy with the layout, sew the blocks into rows always pressing towards the Shoo Fly blocks. Sew the rows together, pinning at every seam intersection to ensure a perfect match.

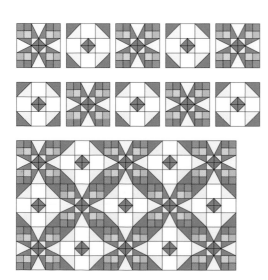

Adding the Borders

25 Sew the seven 1½in wide strips for the inner border into a continuous length. Measure the quilt through the centre from top to bottom. Cut two side borders to this measurement. Pin mark the halves and quarters of one quilt side and one border. Placing right sides together and matching the pins, stitch quilt and border together, easing the quilt side to fit. Repeat on the opposite side and then press. Now measure the quilt through the centre from side to side. Cut two borders to this measurement. Pin and sew to the top and bottom of your quilt and press.

26 Repeat this process to add the outer border, using the seven 4½in wide strips.

27 Your quilt top is now complete. Quilt as desired and bind to finish.

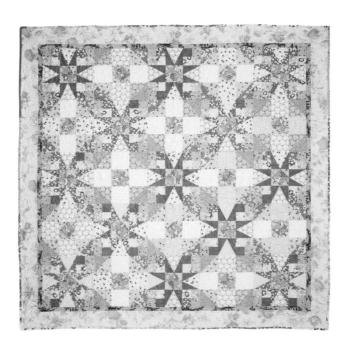

For this lovely quilt we used a selection of fabrics from the California Girl range by Fig Tree Quilts. The shades are gentle and harmonious and create a lovely feminine quilt. The quilt was made by the authors and longarm quilted by The Quilt Room.

Scattered Squares

We wanted to show the versatility of the Multi-Size 2 Peaks in 1 Triangle ruler and for this quilt we created our blocks from half-rectangles using the side triangle on the ruler. Using partial seaming we set the rectangles around a centre square and then sewed flip-over triangles on the corners of the blocks to create the secondary squares. We have given the fabric requirements as three colourways plus background fabric but as you can see our quilt is quite scrappy. If you would like a scrappy effect, you can of course raid your fabric stash to make strips in different fabrics.

Vital Statistics

Size:	54in x 54in
Block size:	12in
Number of blocks:	16
Setting:	4 x 4 blocks, plus 3in border

Requirements

- ½yd (50cm) of aqua fabric
- ⅝yd (60cm) of chocolate fabric
- ½yd (50cm) of apricot fabric
- 2yd (1.75m) of background fabric
- ⅝yd (60cm) of border fabric
- ½yd (50cm) of binding fabric

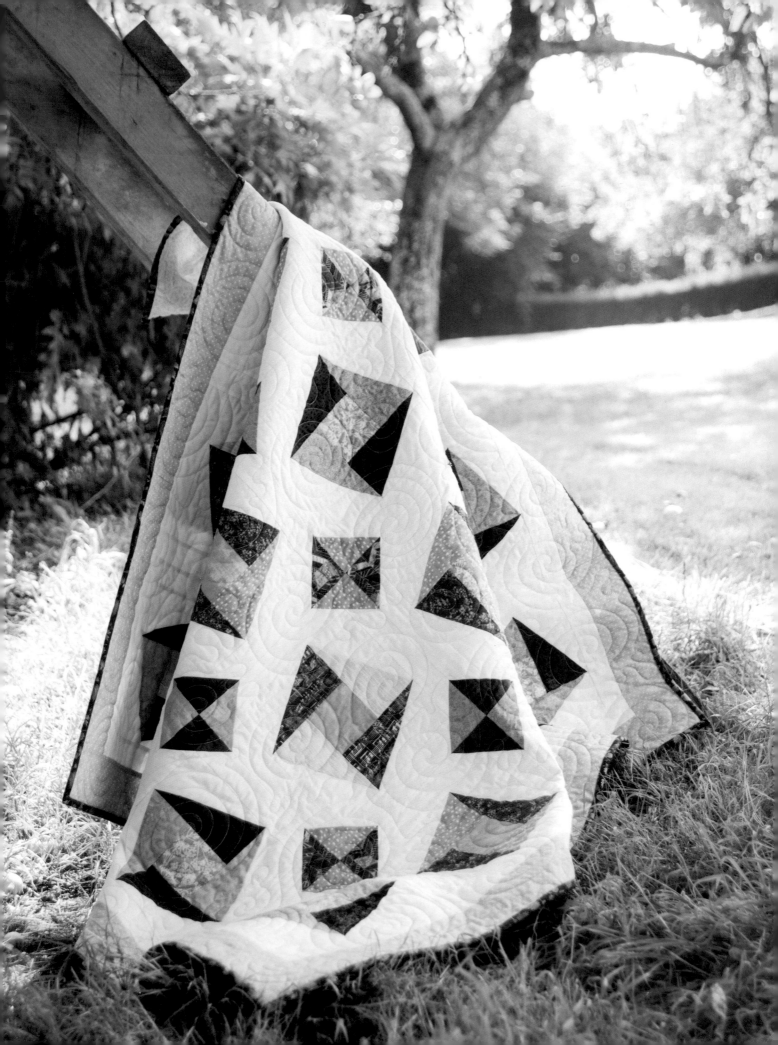

Cutting Instructions

AQUA FABRIC

1 Cut two 6½in strips across the width of the fabric and set aside for the half-rectangle units.

CHOCOLATE FABRIC

2 Cut two 6½in strips across the width of the fabric and set aside for the half-rectangle units.

• Cut two 3½in strips and subcut into eighteen 3½in squares.

APRICOT FABRIC

3 Cut four 3½in strips and subcut into thirty-four 3½in squares.

BACKGROUND FABRIC

4 Cut four 6½in strips across the width of the fabric and set aside for the half-rectangle units.

• Cut nineteen 2in strips across the fabric width and subcut as follows.

– Take eight 2in strips and subcut each strip into four 2in x 9½in rectangles to make a total of thirty-two 2in x 9½in rectangles.
– Take eleven strips and subcut each strip into three 2in x 12½in rectangles to make a total of thirty-two 2in x 12½in rectangles.

BORDER FABRIC

5 Cut six 3½in wide strips across the width of the fabric.

BINDING FABRIC

6 Cut six 2½in wide strips across the width of the fabric.

TIP
You can layer and cut two strips together but make sure they are both *right sides up.*

Making the Half-Rectangle Units

1 Lay one 6½in aqua strip on the cutting mat *right side up.* Place the 2 Peaks in 1 Triangle on the strip as shown in the diagram, lining up the 6½in base line of the ruler with the bottom of the strip. The squared-off top of the triangle will align with the top of the strip. Trim the selvedge and cut the first triangle. Trim the small nubbed-off corner at the base of the triangle, which will help when piecing the triangles into rectangles.

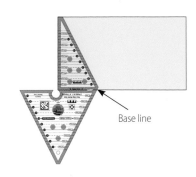

Base line

2 Rotate the ruler 180 degrees to cut the second triangle and continue along the strip, rotating the ruler to cut sixteen triangles. Repeat with the other 6½in aqua strip to make a total of thirty-two aqua triangles.

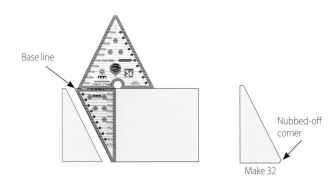

Base line

Nubbed-off corner

Make 32

3 Repeat steps 1 and 2 with the two 6½in chocolate strips to make a total of thirty-two chocolate triangles. These strips should also be cut *right sides up.*

Make 32

4 Repeat steps 1 and 2 with the four 6½in background strips to make a total of sixty-four background triangles. These strips should also be cut *right sides up.*

Make 64

5 Take one aqua triangle and one background triangle and place right sides together, matching the nubbed-off corners. Sew along the diagonal. Open and press the rectangle to the aqua fabric. Repeat to make thirty-two aqua half-rectangle units.

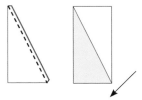

6 Take one chocolate triangle and one background triangle and place right sides together, matching the nubbed-off corners. Sew along the diagonal. Open and press towards the chocolate fabric. Repeat to make thirty-two chocolate half-rectangle units.

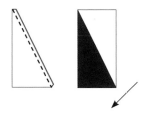

Assembling the Blocks

7 Take two aqua half-rectangle units and two chocolate half-rectangle units and one 3½in apricot square. With right sides together, partially sew one aqua half-rectangle unit along the top of the square as shown, starting the seam approximately in the centre of the 3½in square.

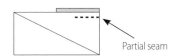

Partial seam

8 Carefully press open towards the aqua half-rectangle unit – this will create a straight edge against which to sew the next half-rectangle unit.

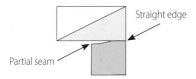

Straight edge

Partial seam

9 Sew a chocolate half-rectangle unit down the right-hand side as shown. Press open.

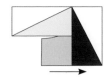

10 Sew an aqua half-rectangle unit along the bottom and then press open as shown.

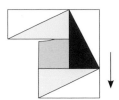

11 Sew a chocolate half-rectangle unit in place and press open. Finish sewing the partial seam to complete the block. Press the work. Repeat to make sixteen blocks.

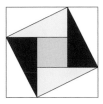

12 Sew a 2in x 9½in background rectangle to both sides of the block and a 2in x 12½in background rectangle to the top and bottom of the block. Press the work. Repeat with all sixteen blocks.

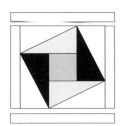

13 Lay out your blocks in four rows of four blocks each, rotating alternate blocks 90 degrees as shown but do not sew them together yet.

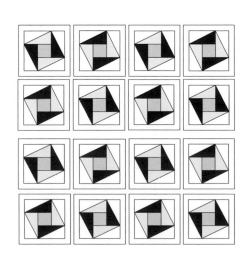

14 Working with the block in the top left-hand corner, take a 3½in apricot square and mark the diagonal on the reverse of the square or mark with a fold. Place it right sides together on the corner of the block as shown and sew along the diagonal.

15 Flip the corner over and press. Once you have checked you have sewn it on accurately, trim the excess fabric to reduce bulk.

16 Repeat with all the blocks, as shown, making sure you are sewing the correct colour flip-over corner in the correct position.

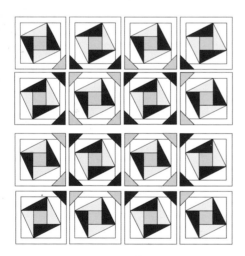

17 Sew the blocks of each row together, pinning at every seam intersection to ensure a perfect match and then sew the rows together. Press the seams in rows one and three in one direction and the seams in rows two and four in the opposite direction, so that the seams nest together nicely when sewn.

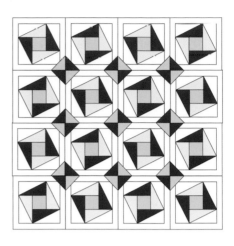

Adding the Border

18 Join the border strips into one continuous length. Determine the vertical measurement from top to bottom through the centre of your quilt top. Cut two borders to this measurement. Mark the halves and quarters of the sides of the quilt and borders with pins. Placing right sides together and matching the pins, stitch the quilt and side borders together, easing the quilt side to fit where necessary. Press the seams.

19 Determine the horizontal measurement across the centre of the quilt top. Cut two borders to this measurement and pin and sew to the top and bottom of your quilt. Press the seams.

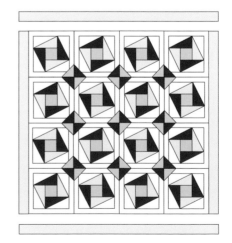

20 Your quilt top is now complete. Quilt as desired and bind to finish.

Now you have learned how to create half-rectangle units quickly and easily you can let your imagination run away with you – it opens up so many design opportunities. This quilt also has a fun backing as the delightful designers from Urban Grey gave us a bundle of their delicious fabrics and we were determined to use absolutely everything! The quilt was made by the authors and longarm quilted by The Quilt Room.

Circular Motion

When we first got the Multi-Size 2 Peaks in 1 Triangle at The Quilt Room all the girls in the shop were very excited about it. Here is Ileana Laws' spectacular quilt that combines the 2 peaks in 1 unit with the half-rectangle units. She used a large-scale print from Amy Butler and she fussy cut some of her strips. We have suggested you allow at least an extra half yard if you are planning to do something similar.

Vital Statistics

Quilt Size:	49½in x 49½in
Block Size:	9in flower blocks
Number of Blocks:	4
Setting:	9in flower blocks with 4½in sashing strips and 4½in border

Requirements

- 1⅛yd (1m) for flower blocks and border – Colour One (see Tip)
- ½yd (0.5m) – Colour Two (green)
- ½yd (0.5m) – Colour Three (dark blue)
- 1¼yd (1.10m) of fabric for background
- ½yd/m of fabric for binding

TIP

If you are going to fussy cut your Colour 1 fabric for the flower blocks and border you should allow at least an extra ½yd/m for this.

Cutting Instructions

COLOUR ONE FABRIC

1 Cut two 2¾in wide strips across the width of the fabric for the four-patch blocks.

- Cut six 5in strips across the width of the fabric.
  - Set four aside for the borders.
  - Two are for the centre triangles in the flower blocks.

COLOUR TWO FABRIC

2 Cut three 2¾in strips across the width of the fabric for the four-patch blocks.

- Cut two 5in strips across the width of the fabric for units A and B.

COLOUR THREE FABRIC

3 Cut one 2¾in wide strip across the width of the fabric for the four-patch blocks.

- Cut two 5in strips across the width of the fabric for units A and B.

BACKGROUND FABRIC

4 Cut eight 5in strips across the width of the fabric.

- Take two and subcut eight 5in x 9½in rectangles.
- Take one and subcut four 5in squares.
- Leave five uncut to use for making side triangles.

BINDING FABRIC

5 Cut five 2½in wide strips across the width of the fabric.

Making the Flower Blocks

1 Take one Colour One 5in strip and, keeping it folded, place the centre triangle of the 2 Peaks in 1 Triangle to the left of the strip. Align the *4½in marked line (5in strip width)* with the bottom of the strip. Cut your first triangle.

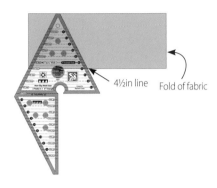

4½in line   Fold of fabric

2 Rotate the triangle 180 degrees and cut the second triangle. Continue to cut four pairs of triangles making a total of eight triangles. Repeat with the second 5in Colour One strip to make another four pairs of triangles. You now have sixteen triangles that will make the four flower blocks using four triangles (petals) for each. Do not discard the excess fabric as this can be used to make the appliqué flower centres.

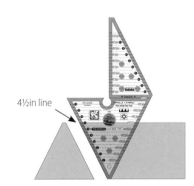

4½in line

3 Take one 5in background strip, *keeping it folded*, and lay the side triangle of the 2 Peaks in 1 Triangle on the strip as shown, aligning the *4½in marked line (5in strip width)* with the bottom of the strip and the cut-off top of the triangle with the top of the strip. Cut one triangle. Note: *Keeping the strip folded is very important when cutting this shape as you need a pair of reverse triangles.*

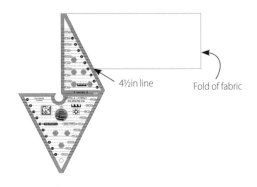

4½in line   Fold of fabric

4 Rotate the triangle 180 degrees and cut the second triangle. Continue to make eight pairs of triangles – sixteen triangles in total. Repeat with another 5in background strip to make a total of thirty-two side triangles – half of these will be reverse triangles.

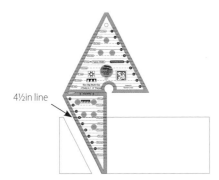

4½in line

5 Sew a side triangle to one side of a Colour One triangle. You will notice that the pieces will appear ¼in out at each end but this is because you have an angled cut. It is important that your pieces are aligned at the top and bottom once sewn, so double check before sewing. Press towards the background fabric.

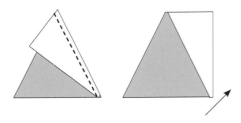

6 Sew a second background triangle to the unit and press towards the background triangle. Repeat with three other petal triangles.

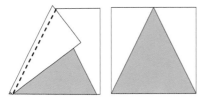

7 Each petal should measure 5in square so check each one and trim to size. If your petals are measuring under 5in then reduce your seam allowance slightly.

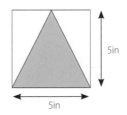

5in

5in

8 Rotate the four petals as shown in the diagram and sew the top two together, pressing the seams to the right. Sew the bottom two together and press the seams to the left. Then sew the pairs together and press. Repeat to make four flowers.

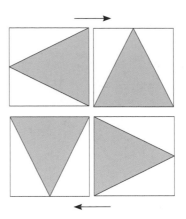

Making the Flower Centres

9 The excess fabric from the 5in flower strips is used to make the flower centres. You need to make four flower centres in total. Cut out a 1½in diameter circle from thin card. Using the card circle as a guide, cut out fabric circles approximately ¼in larger all the way round. Place the card circle on the wrong side of the fabric circle and sew a running stitch around the outside of the card circle. Pull the stitches up tightly around the cardboard circle and knot to hold in place.

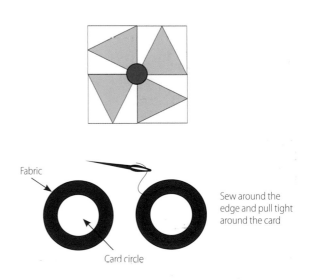

Fabric

Card circle

Sew around the edge and pull tight around the card

10 Press the edge firmly with an iron to crease all round and then carefully remove the cardboard circle. Pin the flower centre right side up in the centre of one of the flowers and appliqué in place with matching thread and small slip stitches. Repeat with all four flowers.

Making the Half-Rectangle Units

11 Lay one 5in Colour Two strip on your cutting mat, *keeping it folded*. Place the 2 Peaks in 1 Triangle on the strip with the *4½in marked line (5in strip width)* at the bottom of the strip. The cut-off top of the triangle will align with the top of the strip. Trim the selvedge and cut the first triangle.

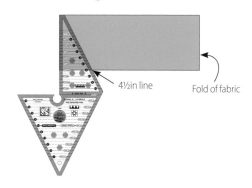

4½in line   Fold of fabric

12 Rotate the triangle 180 degrees and cut the next triangle. Continue along the strip to cut twelve pairs of triangles. Repeat with another 5in Colour Two strip to make a total of twenty-four pairs of triangles – twenty-four triangles and twenty-four reverse triangles.

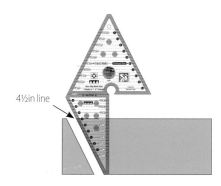

4½in line

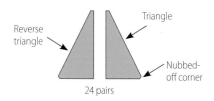

Reverse triangle   Triangle

Nubbed-off corner

24 pairs

> **TIP**
>
> To assist in accurate piecing, when cutting triangles to make half-rectangles it helps to cut off the base diagonal corner. There is a nubbed-off corner at the base of the 2 Peaks in 1 Triangle. After cutting the triangle, move the ruler up so you can trim the nubbed-off corner. This makes for a little more work but ensures accurate piecing.

13 Repeat steps 11 and 12 with two 5in Colour Three strips to make a total of twenty-four pairs of Colour Three triangles.

24 pairs

14 Repeat steps 11 and 12 with three 5in background strips to make a total of thirty-six pairs of background triangles.

36 pairs

15 Take twenty-four Colour Two reverse triangles and twenty-four background reverse triangles and sew along the diagonals to make twenty-four rectangles as shown. Repeat with twelve Colour Two triangles and twelve background triangles to make twelve rectangles. You will have twelve Colour Two triangles spare.

Make 24   Make 12

16 Take twelve Colour Three reverse triangles and twelve background reverse triangles and sew along the diagonals to make twelve rectangles as shown. Repeat with twenty-four Colour Three triangles and twenty-four background reverse triangles to make twenty-four rectangles as shown. You will have twelve Colour Three reverse triangles spare.

Make 12   Make 24

17 Sew the rectangles together as shown in the diagram to make twenty-four unit A and twelve unit B.

Make 24 of Unit A   Make 12 of Unit B

Making the Four-Patch Units

18 Take one 2¾in strip in Colour One and one 2¾in strip in Colour Two and lay right sides together. Sew down the long side. Open and press to the darker fabric. Repeat with the other Colour One and another Colour Two 2¾in strips.

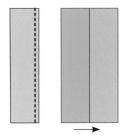

19 With right sides together, lay one strip unit on top of another, rotating the top strip unit 180 degrees. Ensure that the centre seams are neatly aligned. Subcut the units into nine 2¾in wide segments.

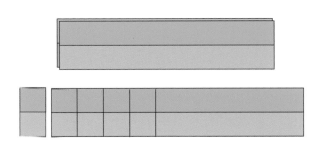

20 Keep the pairs together and sew down the long side as shown. Press open to form nine four-patch units. These are unit C.

Unit C

21 Using the remaining Colour Two 2¾in strip and the Colour Three 2¾in strip, sew down the long side and press to the darker fabric.

22 Cut in half, rotate one half 180 degrees and with right sides together, place one half on top of the other.

23 Subcut into four 2¾in wide segments and keeping the pairs together, sew down the long side to form four corner unit D four-patch units.

Unit D

Assembling the Quilt

24 **Rows 1 and 7:** Take three unit A, two 5in background squares and two 5in x 9½in background rectangles and assemble Row 1 as shown, making sure you are placing the units correctly. Press towards the background fabric. Repeat to make Row 7.

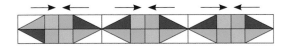

25 **Rows 2, 4 and 6:** Take two unit A, four unit B and three unit C and sew Row 2 making sure you are placing the units correctly. Press towards unit C. Repeat to make Row 4 and Row 6.

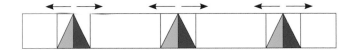

26 **Rows 3 and 5:** Take six unit A, two flower blocks and two 5in x 9½in background rectangles and sew together as shown to make Row 3. Press as shown. Repeat to make Row 5.

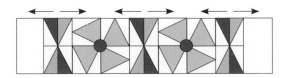

27 Sew the rows together, pinning at every seam intersection to ensure a perfect match.

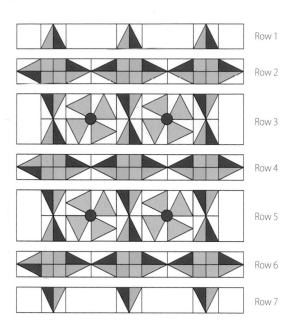

Row 1
Row 2
Row 3
Row 4
Row 5
Row 6
Row 7

29 Sew a unit D to both ends of the remaining two borders and pin and sew to the top and bottom of your quilt. Press the work.

Adding the Border

28 Determine the vertical and horizontal measurements of your quilt. Your quilt is square so both measurements should be the same. Trim four border strips to this measurement. Pin and sew on the side borders and press.

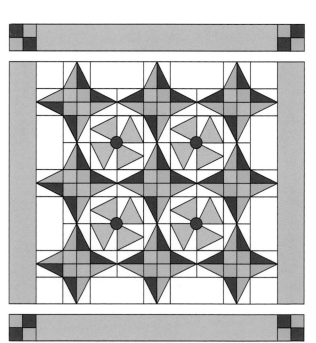

30 Your quilt top is now complete. Quilt as desired and bind to finish.

This quilt uses the ruler to create the 2 peaks in 1 unit and the half-rectangle unit. Combining these units shows just how exciting and intricate your quilts can become. This quilt was made by Ileana Laws and quilted by The Quilt Room.

KALEIDOSCOPE

DOUBLE-STRIP RULER

The Double-Strip Kaleidoscope Ruler is an innovative ruler by Rachel Cross of Creative Grids®. The unique keyhole design really does speed up cutting and allows you to create stunning blocks quickly and easily.

In this next section of the book we show you great ways to use this ruler to its best advantage. Remember, you can use any other kaleidoscope ruler but make sure you are cutting on the correct markings. Using kaleidoscope rulers will not only allow you to make quilts quickly and easily – great for a weekend project – but will leave you feeling inspired and excited and wanting to make more of your own unique projects!

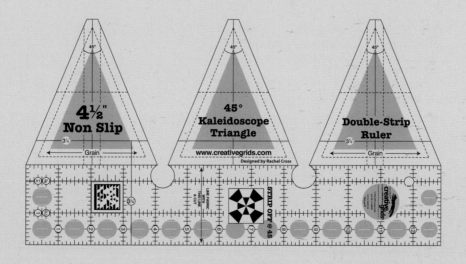

Friday Night

Friday Night and Saturday Morning were the first quilts we made using the brilliant Double-Strip Kaleidoscope Ruler and it was love at first cut! We made this smaller quilt on a Friday night and the larger variation on a Saturday morning – hence the names! The quilts went together beautifully and they look so much more complicated than they really are! They are just perfect for a weekend project.

Vital Statistics

Quilt size:	39in x 39in
Block size:	8in
Number of blocks:	16
Setting:	4 x 4 blocks, plus 3½in wide border (If using fat quarter metres the border can be 4½in wide and the finished quilt will be 41in square)

• •

Requirements

- Four fat quarters in dark colours
- Four fat quarters in light colours
- ½yd (50cm) of binding fabric (1⅝yds/1.5m would be enough for backing and binding)

Cutting Instructions

1 Pair up a light fat quarter with a dark fat quarter. Each pair will make four blocks.

DARK FAT QUARTERS

2 Making sure you are cutting down the 21in length, cut each of the four dark fat quarters into the following.

- Two 4½in x 21in strips.
- Two 4in x 21in strips.

Set the eight 4in strips aside for the border.

Note: for those using fat quarter *metres* cut as follows.

- Two 4½in x 21in strips.
- Two 5in x 21in strips.

Set the eight 5in strips aside for the border.

LIGHT FAT QUARTERS

3 Making sure you are cutting down the 21in length, cut each of the four light fat quarters into the following.

- Two 4½in x 21in strips.
- Two 3¼in x 21in strips. Subcut each of the two 3¼in strips into four 3¼in squares. Now cut diagonally in half to create sixteen corner triangles from each fat quarter.

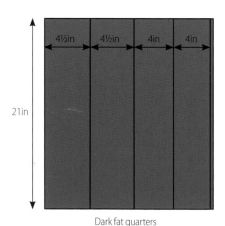

Dark fat quarters

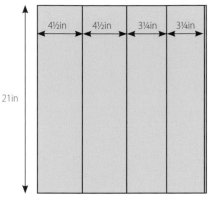

Light fat quarters

TIP There is a 3¼in line and square marked on the ruler, making cutting these corner triangles very easy.

BINDING FABRIC

4 Cut five 2½in strips across the width of the fabric.

Making the Blocks

1 Working with one pair of light and dark fabrics at a time, take one light 4½in strip and one dark 4½in strip and press right sides together, ensuring that they are *exactly* one on top of the other. The pressing will help hold the two strips together.

4½in strips

2 Lay them out on a cutting mat and trim the selvedge. Position the Double-Strip Kaleidoscope ruler as shown in the diagram. Holding the ruler firmly in place, cut the first triangle. Continue cutting along the strip, moving the ruler when necessary. You need to cut eight pairs of triangles in total.

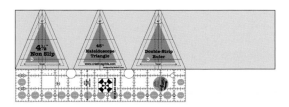

3 Repeat with the other pair of 4½in strips from the same fabric to make a total of sixteen pairs of triangles.

4 Keep the pairs together and take them to the sewing machine. Sew each pair together down one side. Chain piecing will speed this up.

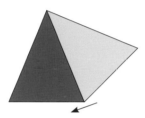

5 Open the sixteen pairs of triangles and press towards the left.

6 Sew these sixteen units into pairs to make eight half blocks. Chain piece to save time and press to the left.

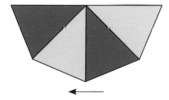

7 Sew two half blocks together to form one kaleidoscope, pinning at the centre seam intersection to ensure a perfect match. Press the seam.

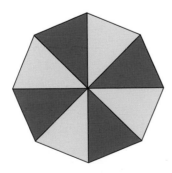

8 Take four light corner triangles from the same fabric and sew to the four dark triangles as shown, to square up the block. Make sure the triangle is centred before sewing and then press open. Repeat to make four blocks from this pair of fat quarters.

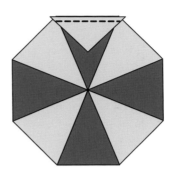

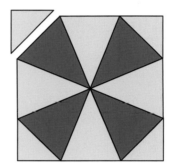

9 Using an 8½in quilting square if you have one, trim the square to size. It should measure 8½in x 8½in.

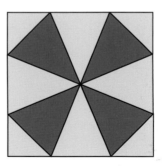

10 Repeat steps 1–9 with the three other pairs of fat quarters to make a total of sixteen blocks.

Assembling the Quilt

11 Lay out the blocks into four rows of four blocks. We chose to have four blocks of the same fabric in the centre but you can arrange them how you like. When you are happy with the layout, sew the blocks into rows and then sew the rows together. Press alternate rows in opposite directions so the seams will nest together nicely when sewing the rows together. Pin at every seam intersection to ensure a perfect match. Press the work.

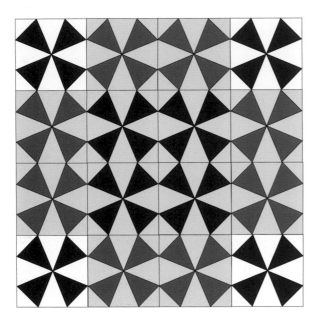

Adding the Border

12 Join the eight border strips into a continuous length. Determine the vertical measurement from top to bottom through the centre of your quilt top. Cut two side borders to this measurement. Mark the halves and quarters of one quilt side and one border with pins. Placing right sides together and matching the pins, stitch the quilt and border together, easing the quilt side to fit where necessary. Repeat on the opposite side. Press the seams.

13 Now determine the horizontal measurement from side to side across the centre of the quilt top. Cut two borders to this measurement. Pin and sew to the top and bottom of your quilt and press.

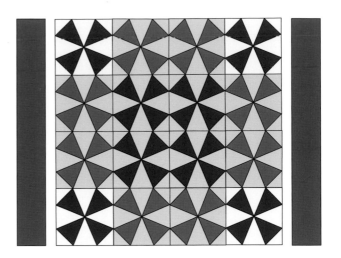

14 Your quilt top is now complete. Quilt as desired and bind to finish.

For this quilt we used the gorgeous French General range called Rouenneries Deux, with its lovely array of faded reds and muted creams. The quilt was made by the authors and longarm quilted by The Quilt Room.

Saturday Morning

Saturday Morning is our larger variation of the Friday Night quilt design. The construction of the blocks is the same as the Friday Night quilt, however the cutting instructions differ slightly. We used assorted Thirties reproduction fabrics together with a white-on-white fabric to give the quilt a gorgeous fresh look.

Vital Statistics

Quilt Size:	52in x 68in
Block Size:	8in
Number of Blocks:	48
Setting:	6 x 8 blocks plus 2in wide border

Requirements

- Eight fat quarters in assorted Thirties reproduction fabrics (binding included)
- 2¾yd (2.6m) white-on-white fabric

Cutting Instructions

THIRTIES FAT QUARTERS

1 Making sure that you are cutting down the 21in length, cut each of the eight fat quarters into the following.

- Three 4½in x 21in strips.
- Two 2½in x 21in strips for the scrappy binding.

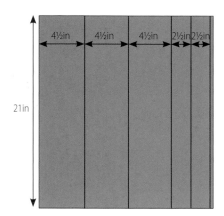

WHITE FABRIC

2 Cut twelve 4½in wide strips across the width of the fabric. Cut in half to make twenty-four rectangles 4½in x 21in.

- Cut eight 3¼in strips and subcut each strip into twelve 3¼in squares to make ninety-six squares. Subcut each 3¼in square in half diagonally to make 192 corner triangles.
- Cut six 2½in strips across the width of the fabric for the border.

Making the Blocks

1 We chose to make our blocks scrappy but you could sew each block using one fabric. Working with one pair of white and Thirties fabrics at a time, take one white 4½in wide strip and one Thirties 4½in wide strip and press right sides together, ensuring that they are *exactly* one on top of the other. The pressing will help hold the two strips together.

2 Lay the strips out on a cutting mat and trim the selvedge. Position the Double-Strip Kaleidoscope ruler as shown in the diagram. Holding the ruler firmly in place, cut the first triangle. Continue cutting along the strip, moving the ruler when necessary. You need to cut eight triangles.

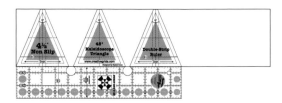

3 Keep the pairs together and take them to the sewing machine. Sew each pair together down one side. Chain piecing will speed this up.

4 Open the eight pairs of triangles and press towards the left. At this point you could start sewing the pairs into half blocks if you wanted your kaleidoscope blocks to be made from the same fabric. However, we wanted scrappy kaleidoscope blocks so it is necessary to sew all your pairs of triangles before sewing the half blocks together.

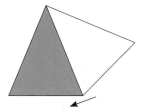

5 Repeat with all twenty-four pairs of 4½in strips to make a total of 192 pairs of triangles. Chain piecing will speed up this process.

6 Sew these 192 units into pairs to make ninety-six half blocks, trying not to sew pairs of the same fabric together. Chain piece to save time and press to the left.

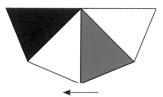

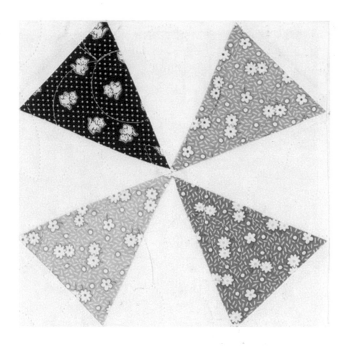

7 Sew two half blocks together to form one kaleidoscope, pinning at the centre seam intersection to ensure a perfect match. Press the seam. Repeat to make forty-eight blocks.

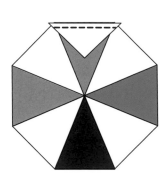

9 Using an 8½in quilting square if you have one, trim the square to size. It should measure 8½in x 8½in.

8 Take four white corner triangles and sew to the four Thirties triangles of the kaleidoscope as shown, to square up the block. Make sure the triangle is centred before sewing and then press open.

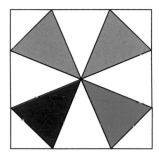

10 Repeat steps 8 and 9 to add white corner triangles to all kaleidoscope blocks to make a total of forty-eight blocks.

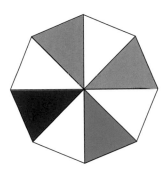

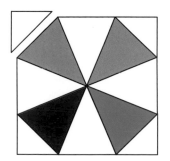

Assembling the Quilt

11 Sew the blocks into eight rows of six blocks each, pinning at every seam intersection to ensure a perfect match.

13 Determine the horizontal measurement from side to side across the centre of the quilt top. Cut two borders to this measurement. Pin and sew to the top and bottom of your quilt and press.

Adding the Border

12 Join the six 2½in white border strips into a continuous length. Determine the vertical measurement from top to bottom through the centre of your quilt top. Cut two side borders to this measurement. Mark the halves and quarters of one quilt side and one border with pins. Placing right sides together and matching the pins, stitch the quilt and border together, easing the quilt side to fit where necessary. Repeat on the opposite side. Press the seams.

14 Your quilt top is now complete. Quilt as desired and bind to finish. To make a scrappy binding, sew thirteen of the 2½in strips set aside for the binding into a continuous length. You need approximately 250in.

We loved the scrappy effect created by mixing up all the fabrics in the quilt. You could have the same fabrics in each kaleidoscope block and this would create a totally different but equally stunning quilt. The quilt was made by the authors and longarm quilted by The Quilt Room on their Gammill Statler Stitcher.

Misty Mountain

In our Friday Night and Saturday Morning quilts we made sure the light triangles in our block matched up with the adjoining ones in the next block. This created light diamonds and squares as secondary designs. In our elegant Misty Mountain variation we have done the reverse and designed the light and dark triangles to be sewn together.

Vital Statistics

Quilt Size:	57in x 73in
Block Size:	8in
Number of Blocks:	48
Setting:	6 x 8 blocks, plus 4½in wide border

• •

Requirements

- One fat quarter each of lightest Colours 1 and 2
- One fat quarter each of light Colours 3 and 4
- ½yd (50cm) each of medium Colours 5 and 6
- ½yd (50cm) each of medium/dark Colours 7 and 8
- ½yd (50cm) each of dark Colours 9 and 10
- 1yd (1m) of fabric for border
- ½yd (50cm) of fabric for binding

Sorting the Fabrics

Pair up the fat quarters of Colours 1 and 2, then the fat quarters of Colours 3 and 4. Cut the ½yds of Colours 5 and 6 into fat quarters and pair them up. Repeat with the ½yds of Colours 7 and 8 and Colours 9 and 10. Each pair of fat quarters will make six blocks.

Cutting Instructions

BLOCK FABRICS

1 Take the fat quarters of Colours 1 and 2 and place them right sides together. Press lightly to hold them together. Making sure you are cutting down the 21in length, cut the following strips.

- Three 4½in x 21in strips.
- One 3¼in x 21in strip.

Set the three 4½in pairs of strips aside for the moment, keeping the pairs carefully together.

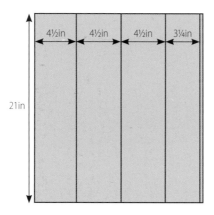

2 Take the 3¼in pair of strips and subcut into six 3¼in squares. Subcut across the squares diagonally, to create twelve Colour 1 corner triangles and twelve Colour 2 corner triangles.

- Repeat with all the pairs of fat quarters, keeping the strips of each pair of colours together.

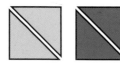

BORDER FABRIC

3 Cut seven 5in wide strips across the width of the fabric.

BINDING FABRIC

4 Cut seven 2½in wide strips across the width of the fabric.

Making the Blocks

1 Working with one pair of 4½in strips from Colours 1 and 2 at a time, lay them out on a cutting mat. Place the Double-Strip Kaleidoscope Ruler as far to the left of the strip as possible and cut eight triangles, moving the ruler along the strip as necessary. Repeat with all three pairs of 4½in strips from Colours 1 and 2 to make a total of twenty-four pairs of triangles. (For clarity our diagrams show Colours 7 and 8.)

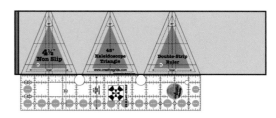

2 Now sew each pair of triangles together down one side, chain piecing for speed.

3 Open the twenty-four pairs and press the seams to the left.

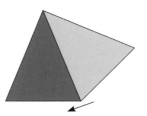

4 Sew these twenty-four units into pairs to make twelve half blocks. Chain piece to save time and then press to the left.

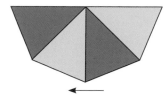

5 Sew two half blocks together to form one kaleidoscope, pinning at the centre seam intersection to ensure a perfect match. Press the seam. Repeat to make six of these units.

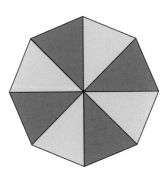

6 Take four Colour 1 corner triangles and sew to four Colour 2 triangles to square up the block. Make sure the triangle is centred before sewing. Open and press to the corner triangle. Repeat this process to make three of these blocks.

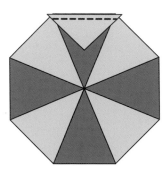

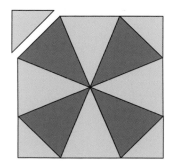

7 Sew four Colour 2 corner triangles to four Colour 1 triangles. Repeat to make three of these blocks. Using an 8½in quilting square if you have one, trim the blocks to size. They should measure 8½in x 8½in. You now have six blocks in Colours 1 and 2.

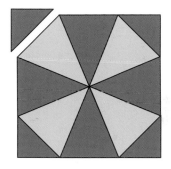

8 Repeat the above steps with Colours 3 and 4 to create six blocks. Then, with the remaining pairs of colours, create twelve blocks each from Colours 5 and 6, 7 and 8, 9 and 10.

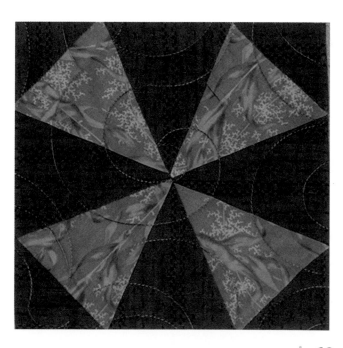

Assembling the Quilt

9 Lay out the blocks as shown in the diagram, grading the colours from bottom right to top left and alternating the blocks in the same colourways. Always make sure you are positioning a block with dark corners next to a block with light corners.

10 When you are happy with the layout, sew the blocks into rows and then sew the rows together. Press the blocks in Row 1 to the left and the blocks in Row 2 to the right, so that the seams nest together nicely when the rows are sewn together. Pin at every seam intersection to ensure a perfect match.

Row 1
Row 2
Row 3
Row 4
Row 5
Row 6
Row 7
Row 8

Colours 9 and 10
Colours 7 and 8
Colours 5 and 6
Colours 3 and 4
Colours 1 and 2

Adding the Border

11 Join the seven border strips into a continuous length. Determine the vertical measurement from top to bottom through the centre of your quilt top. Cut two side borders to this measurement.

12 Mark the halves and quarters of one quilt side and one border with pins. Placing right sides together and matching the pins, stitch the quilt and border together, easing the quilt side to fit where necessary. Repeat on the opposite side. Press the work.

13 Determine the horizontal measurement from side to side across the centre of the quilt top. Cut two borders to this measurement. Pin and sew to the top and bottom of your quilt and press.

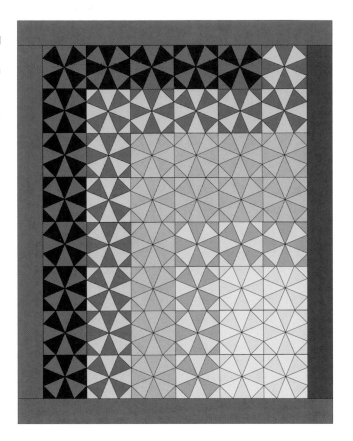

14 Your quilt top is now complete. Quilt as desired and bind to finish.

The same kaleidoscope block can look so different just by grading the colours from light to dark, as you can see in this dramatic quilt. The quilt was made by the authors and longarm quilted by The Quilt Room on their Gammill Statler Stitcher.

Playtime

This is such a pretty quilt and so quick and easy to make. The fabric choices are easy too, as you only have to choose three fabrics. One of the fabrics is also used as the border fabric and another is also used for the binding. It would make a great play mat for a child or a cosy lap quilt for a teenager to snuggle under when away from home.

Vital Statistics

Quilt Size:	50in x 58½in
Block Size:	8in
Number of Blocks:	20
Setting:	4 x 5 blocks with 5½in striped sashing and 5in plain border

• •

Requirements

- 1½yd (1.4m) of Colour 1 (red) – includes binding
- 1yd (80cm) of Colour 2 (pink)
- 1½yd (1.4m) of Colour 3 (coffee) – includes border

Cutting Instructions

COLOUR 1 (RED)

1 Cut five 4½in strips across the width of the fabric.

- Cut six 1½in strips across the width of the fabric.
- Cut six 2½in wide strips across the width of the fabric and set aside for the binding.

COLOUR 2 (PINK)

2 Cut five 4½in strips across the width of the fabric.

- Cut three 2in strips across the width of the fabric.

COLOUR 3 (COFFEE)

3 Cut four 3¼in strips across the width of the fabric. Subcut each strip into ten 3¼in squares. Subcut all forty squares diagonally to create eighty corner triangles.

- Cut six 1½in strips across the width of the fabric.
- Cut five 5½in strips across the width of the fabric and set aside for the outer border.

Making the Blocks

1 Take a 4½in Colour 1 strip and a 4½in Colour 2 strip and lay them right sides together on a cutting mat, aligning the edges.

2 Position the Double-Strip Kaleidoscope Ruler as far to the left as possible and cut out the triangles. Continue cutting along the strip, moving the ruler when necessary. You need to cut sixteen triangles. Repeat with all five Colour 1 and five Colour 2 4½in strips to make a total of eighty pairs of triangles.

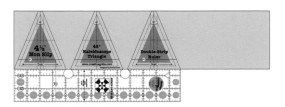

3 Keep the pairs together and take to the sewing machine. Sew each pair together down one side. Chain piecing will speed this up.

4 Open the eighty pairs and press the seams to the left.

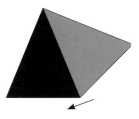

5 Sew these eighty units into pairs to make forty half blocks. Chain piece to save time and then press to the left.

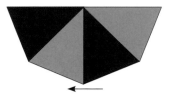

6 Sew two half blocks together to form one kaleidoscope, pinning at every seam intersection to ensure a perfect match. Press the seam. Repeat to make twenty of these units.

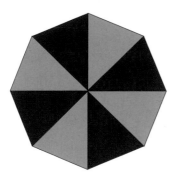

7 Take four Colour 3 corner triangles and sew to four Colour 2 segments to square up the block. Make sure the triangle is centred before sewing. Press open. Repeat to make twelve of block A.

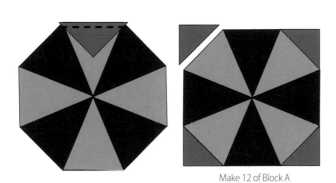

Make 12 of Block A

8 Repeat step 7, sewing Colour 3 corner triangles to four Colour 1 segments. Repeat to make eight of block B.

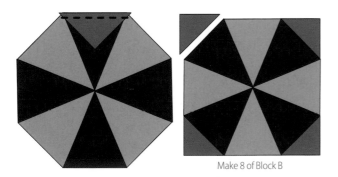

Make 8 of Block B

9 Using an 8½in quilting square if you have one, trim all twenty blocks to size. They should measure 8½in x 8½in.

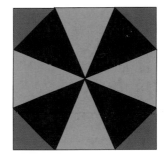

Making the Sashing Strips

10 Sew a 2in Colour 2 strip together with two 1½in Colour 1 strips and two 1½in Colour 3 strips into a strip unit as shown. Press in one direction. Repeat to make three strip units.

Colour 3
Colour 1
Colour 2

Assembling the Quilt

11 Sew three block A and two block B together, alternating the blocks as shown to make one row. Repeat to make four rows.

12 Measure the width of the rows and trim the three sashing strips to this measurement. They will measure approximately 40½in. It is important that all three sashing strips measure the same.

13 Pin and sew the sashing strips to the rows as shown. Press towards the sashing strips.

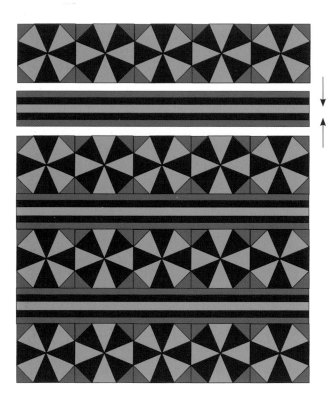

Adding the Border

14 Determine the horizontal measurement from side to side through the centre of your quilt top. Cut two borders to this measurement.

15 Mark the halves and quarters of the top of the quilt and one border with pins. Placing right sides together and matching the pins, stitch the quilt and border together, easing the quilt side to fit where necessary. Repeat on the bottom of the quilt.

16 Join the remaining three border strips together. Determine the vertical measurement through the centre of the quilt top. Cut two side borders to this measurement. Pin and sew to the sides of your quilt and then press.

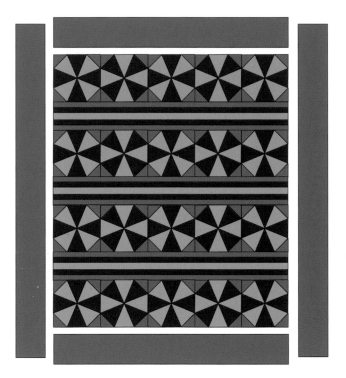

17 Your quilt top is now complete. Quilt as desired and bind to finish.

Bold, vibrant reds make for a colourful, fun quilt that would brighten any room or could be used for a special baby's play mat. Made by the authors and longarm quilted by The Quilt Room on their Gammill Statler Stitcher.

Two to Tango

This is a versatile pattern that is easy to adjust into a quilt of whatever size you need. All you need to know is that two fat quarters – one light and one dark – will make five blocks and in our quilt that is one row. No wastage and no fuss. If you want to increase the size of the quilt just pick up another pair of fat quarters to make another five blocks – now that really is simple.

Vital Statistics

Quilt Size:	48in x 48in
Block Size:	8in
Number of Blocks:	25
Setting:	5 x 5 blocks, plus 4in border

Requirements

- Five fat quarters in dark colours
- Five fat quarters in light colours
- ¾yd (70cm) of fabric for border
- ½yd (50cm) of fabric for binding

Cutting Instructions

LIGHT AND DARK FAT QUARTERS

1 Pair up a light fat quarter with a dark fat quarter. Each pair will make five blocks.

- Take one pair of light and dark fat quarters and place right sides together. Press lightly to hold them together. Making sure you are cutting down the 21in length, cut the following strips.

  - Five 2½in x 21in strips.
  - One 3¼in x 21in strip.

- Set the five 2½in pairs of strips aside for the moment keeping the five pairs carefully together.

2 Take the 3¼in pair of strips and subcut into six 3¼in squares. Subcut across the squares diagonally, to create twelve light corner triangles and twelve dark corner triangles.

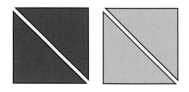

3 Repeat this with all five pairs of light and dark fat quarters. We recommend working with just one pair of fat quarters at a time to make one row.

BORDER FABRIC

4 Cut five 4½in wide strips across the width of the fabric.

BINDING FABRIC

5 Cut five 2½in wide strips across the width of the fabric.

Making the Blocks

1 Working with one pair of fat quarters at a time, take one pair of light and dark 2½in strips and sew down the long side as shown. Press towards the dark fabric. Repeat with all five pairs of 2½in strips. Your strip units should measure 4½in and if they do not then you must adjust your seam allowance.

2 Place two strips units right sides together, rotating one strip unit 180 degrees as shown in the diagram. Make sure the edges and the centre seams are neatly aligned.

3 Position the Double-Strip Kaleidoscope Ruler as far to the left as possible, as shown in the diagram and cut the triangles. Continue cutting along the strip, moving the ruler when necessary. You need to cut eight pairs of triangles.

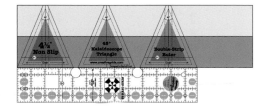

4 Sew each pair together down one side. It is important to always sew down the same side of your pairs so, as a guide, make sure the dark fabric of your top triangle is always in the same place. Chain piece to save time and thread.

5 Open the eight pairs and press all seams to the left, as shown.

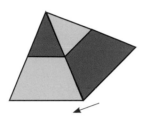

6 Sew these eight units into pairs to make four half blocks. Chain piece to save time and then press to the left.

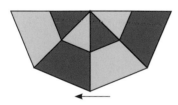

7 Your seams should nest together nicely. Repeat to make two kaleidoscope units. Press the seams.

8 Repeat steps 2–7 with two other strip units to make another two blocks.

9 Cut the fifth strip unit on its own and use the eight triangles to make one block. Make sure to alternate the lights and darks when sewing the triangles together. You now have five kaleidoscope units from this pair of fat quarters.

10 Take four light corner triangles and sew to a section with the dark fabric on the outside to square up the block. Make sure the corner triangle is centred before sewing. Press open. Repeat to make two of these blocks.

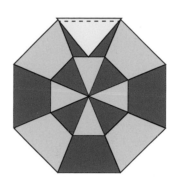
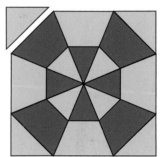

11 Take four dark corner triangles and sew to a section with the light fabric on the outside to square up the block. Make sure the corner triangle is centred before sewing. Press open. Repeat to make three of these blocks. You now have three blocks with dark corner triangles and two blocks with light corner triangles and four light triangles spare.

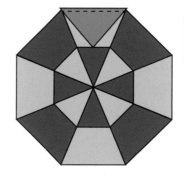
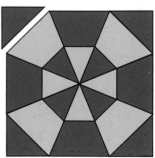

12 Using an 8½in quilting square if you have one, trim the squares to size. They should measure 8½in x 8½in.

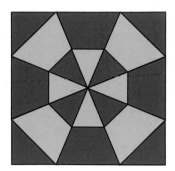

13 Sew the five blocks together, alternating the blocks with light and dark corners, pinning at every seam intersection to ensure a perfect match. Press the seams towards the blocks that have dark corners. You have now made one row.

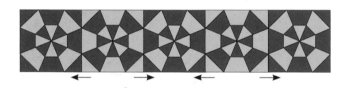

14 Repeat steps 1–13 to make four further rows, always pressing seams towards the blocks with dark corners. Rows two and four need to have three blocks with light corners and two blocks with dark corners. If you are undecided on the placement of your rows you can leave sewing the corners on the fifth blocks of each row until you know where each row will be placed.

TIP

Save time and thread by having a small rectangle of scrap fabric by your machine and always run your machine onto it when you come to the end of a line of sewing. Keep this under your presser foot until you are ready to sew again and you therefore won't have to hang on to the ends of your thread when starting to sew.

Assembling the Quilt

15 Sew the rows together, alternating the rows that have three blocks with dark corners with the rows that have three blocks with light corners. Pin at every seam intersection. Press the work.

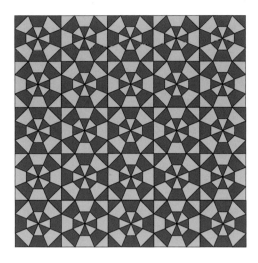

Adding the Border

16 Determine the vertical measurement from to bottom through the centre of your quilt top. Cut two side borders to this measurement. Mark the halves and quarters of one quilt side and one border with pins. Placing them right sides together and matching the pins, stitch the quilt and border together, easing the quilt side to fit where necessary. Repeat on the opposite side.

17 Join the remaining three border strips together. Determine the horizontal measurement from side to side across the centre of the quilt top. Cut two borders to this measurement. Pin and sew these borders to the top and bottom of your quilt and press.

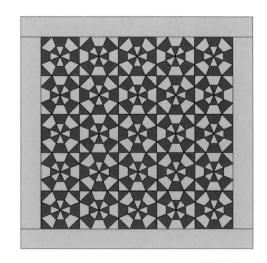

18 Your quilt top is now complete. Quilt as desired and bind to finish.

You can use jelly roll strips to make the kaleidoscope blocks in this quilt but you do need 3¼in wide strips for the corner triangles. There are lots of design opportunities to think about! Made by the authors and longarm quilted by The Quilt Room.

Jubilee

This quilt pattern is a good one for using up assorted strips of fabric as it looks great scrappy. You could, of course, opt for a more coordinated look by having just two colourways for the kaleidoscope and chain blocks. The quilt is set on point, adding a new dimension, and we have mixed our kaleidoscope blocks with chain blocks and plain squares.

Vital Statistics

Quilt Size:	58in x 70in
Block Size:	8in
Number of Blocks:	18 Kaleidoscope, 12 Chain and 20 solid blocks
Setting:	On point

Requirements

- Ten assorted 4½in wide strips cut across the width of the fabric *
- Four assorted 2½in wide strips cut across the width of the fabric *
- 3¼yd (3m) of fabric for background
- ½yd (50cm) of fabric for binding

* If using just two colourways
- 1yd (75cm) of Colour 1, cut into five 4½in wide strips and two 2½in wide strips
- 1yd (75cm) of Colour 2, cut into five 4½in wide strips and two 2½in wide strips

Sorting the Fabrics

Pair up the ten assorted 4½in wide strips into five pairs of strips, or if you are using just two colours pair up a 4½in strip from each colourway. Each pair will make four blocks.

Cutting Instructions

BACKGROUND FABRIC

1 Cut two 2½in wide strips across the width of the fabric.

- Cut two 4½in wide strips across the width of the fabric.
- Cut two 6½in wide strips across the width of the fabric.

  – Cut three 3¼in wide strips across the width of the fabric and subcut each strip into twelve 3¼in squares to make thirty-six squares. Subcut across the squares diagonally to create seventy-two triangles for the corners of the kaleidoscope blocks.

- Cut five 8½in wide strips across the width of the fabric. Subcut each strip into four 8½in squares to make a total of twenty 8½in squares.
- Cut two 13½in wide strips across the width of the fabric and subcut each strip into three 13½in squares. Take five of the 13½in squares and cut across both diagonals to make twenty setting triangles. You need eighteen, so two triangles are spare.

- Cut one 7¾in wide strips across the width of the fabric and cut two 7¾in squares. Cut across one diagonal of each square to form four corner triangles. Cutting the setting and corner triangles this way ensures the outer edges of your quilt are not on the bias.

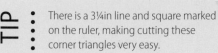

TIP There is a 3¼in line and square marked on the ruler, making cutting these corner triangles very easy.

BINDING FABRIC

2 Cut seven 2½in wide strips across the width of the fabric.

Making the Kaleidoscope Blocks

1 Working with one pair of 4½in strips at a time, lay the pair of strips right sides together on a cutting mat. Position the Double-Strip Kaleidoscope Ruler as far to the left as possible and cut the first triangle. Continue cutting along the strip, moving the ruler when necessary. You need to cut sixteen pairs of triangles.

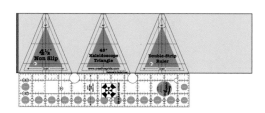

2 Keep the pairs together and take to the sewing machine. Sew each pair together down one side, making sure you always sew down the same side of each pair.

3 Open the sixteen pairs and press the seams to the left as shown in the diagram.

4 Sew these sixteen units into pairs to make eight half blocks and press towards the left. Chain piece to save time.

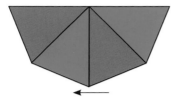

5 Sew two half blocks together to form one kaleidoscope pinning at the centre seam intersection to ensure a perfect match. Press the seam. Repeat to make four kaleidoscopes.

6 Take four corner triangles and sew to either four light triangles or four dark triangles to square up the block (see Tip). Make sure the triangle is centred before sewing. Press open. Repeat to make four blocks like this.

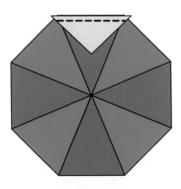

> **TIP**
>
> When deciding where you are going to sew the corner triangles, remember that your blocks are eventually placed on point and sewing the corners to the lighter fabric often works best.

7 Using an 8½in quilting square if you have one, trim the blocks to size. They should measure 8½in x 8½in.

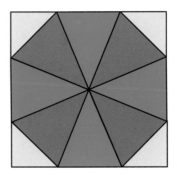

Making the Chain Blocks

8 Take a 2½in coloured strip and sew to the long side of a 6½in background strip to make strip unit A. Press as shown. Repeat to make two of these units. Cut each strip unit into sixteen segments to make a total of thirty-two segments. Twenty-four are needed, so eight are spare.

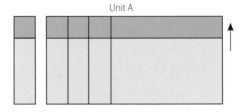

Unit A

9 Take a 2½in coloured strip and sew between a 2½in background strip and a 4½in background strip to make strip unit B. Press as shown. Repeat to make two of these units. Cut each strip unit into sixteen segments to make a total of thirty-two segments. Twenty-four are needed, so eight are spare.

Unit B

10 Sew a segment from strip unit A to a segment from strip unit B as shown, pinning at every seam intersection to ensure a perfect match. Press the seams. Make twenty-four of these units.

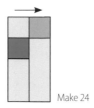

Make 24

11 Take two units and rotate one 180 degrees. Sew together, pinning at every seam intersection to ensure a perfect match. Press the seams. Make twelve blocks in total.

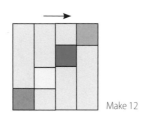

Make 12

Assembling the Quilt

12 Referring to the quilt diagram, lay out the blocks as shown. Sew a setting triangle to each side of a kaleidoscope block to create Row 1. The setting triangles have been cut slightly larger to make the blocks 'float', so when sewing the setting triangles make sure the bottom of the triangle is aligned with the block. Press as shown. Continue to sew the blocks together to form rows with setting triangles at each end. Always press towards the kaleidoscope or chain block as this will ensure your seams are going in different directions when sewing the rows together.

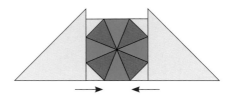

13 Sew the rows together, pinning at every intersection, and sew the corner triangles on last.

14 Your quilt top is now complete. Quilt as desired and bind to finish.

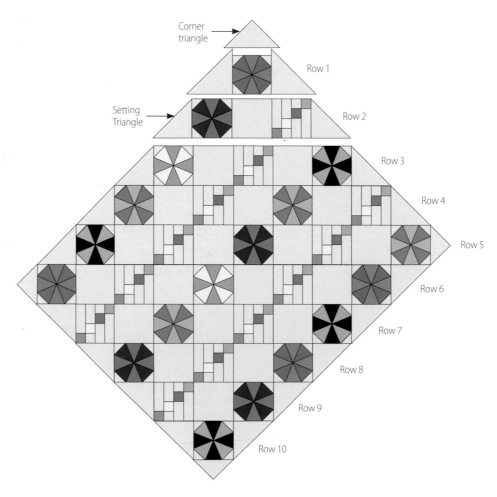

Corner triangle

Row 1

Setting Triangle

Row 2

Row 3

Row 4

Row 5

Row 6

Row 7

Row 8

Row 9

Row 10

These jewel-like fabrics by Philip Jacobs for Westminster Fabrics were the perfect choice for our Jubilee quilt to celebrate Queen Elizabeth's Diamond Jubilee. Made by the authors and longarm quilted by The Quilt Room.

FLYING GEESE

MULTI-SIZE TRIANGLE RULER

The Multi-Size Flying Geese & 45°/90° Triangle from Creative Grids enables you to make the traditional flying geese unit easily and accurately in sizes from 1in x 2in to 6in x 12in. The 90 degree triangle also enables you to make quarter-square triangles from strips and the 45 degree triangle enables you to make half-square triangles from strips, which makes this ruler very useful indeed!

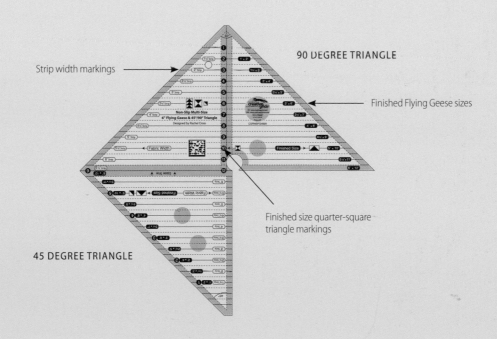

Strip width markings

90 DEGREE TRIANGLE

Finished Flying Geese sizes

Finished size quarter-square triangle markings

45 DEGREE TRIANGLE

The Flying Geese Unit

The flying geese unit is made up of a 90 degree centre triangle with a 45 degree triangle on each side. It is important to understand the difference between a 90 degree triangle and a 45 degree triangle as they look pretty similar.

When cutting at any 45 degree angle you create a bias edge and bias edges tend to stretch if not handled with care. Many people use spray starch to stabilize bias edges when sewing and, although we don't tend to do this, it can be very helpful. One thing you should always remember is to press bias edges gently and never use steam. The important thing however is that you don't end up with outer bias edges. The aim is always to have straight edges on the outside edges of your blocks.

The 90 degree centre triangle of a flying geese unit has straight edges top and bottom and bias edges on the sides. The 45 degree side triangles, however, have straight edges on the two sides that form the outside of the unit. The bias edge of the 45 degree triangle is sewn to the bias edge of the centre triangle. Mission accomplished – we have a unit that has straight edges on all four sides when sewn.

Study the diagrams here, which show the bias and straight edges, to explain the angles of the triangles in the flying geese block.

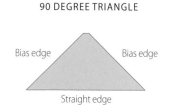

90 DEGREE TRIANGLE

Bias edge   Bias edge

Straight edge

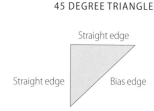

45 DEGREE TRIANGLE

Straight edge

Straight edge   Bias edge

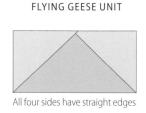

FLYING GEESE UNIT

All four sides have straight edges

1 When using the 90 degree triangle for the centres of the flying geese units, align the correct strip width line along the bottom of the strip and the cut off top of the triangle along the top. Cut the first triangle.

2 Rotate the ruler 180 degrees and cut the next triangle. Continue along the strip to cut the required number of triangles.

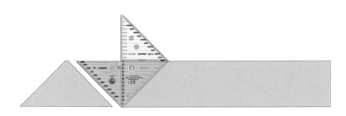

3 When using the 45 degree triangle for the side triangles of the flying geese units, *fold the fabric strip in half*. This enables you to cut the right and left triangles at the same time. Align the correct strip width line along the bottom of the strip and the cut off top of the triangle along the top. Cut the first pair of triangles.

Fold of fabric

4 Rotate the ruler 180 degrees and cut the next pair of triangles. Continue along the strip to cut the required number of triangles. Note the keyhole gap that allows this cutting.

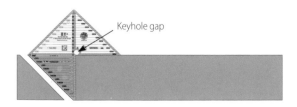

Keyhole gap

5 Notice that the 90 degree centre triangle has a cut off top and the 45 degree triangles have one cut off point.

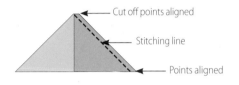

6 When sewing the half-square triangles to the centre triangles make sure you always have the cut off points matching. They will match either on the right side of the centre triangle or on the left side.

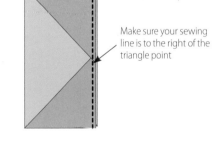

Cut off points aligned

Stitching line

Points aligned

7 When sewing two flying geese units together the stitching line must be to the right of the point so you don't cut off the tip of the triangle.

Make sure your sewing line is to the right of the triangle point

Flight to Paradise

In our Flight to Paradise quilt we have used virtually every measurement there is on our Creative Grids Multi-Size Flying Geese & 45°/90° Triangle. We couldn't resist trying out all the sizes to see what they looked like and then decided they looked quite interesting altogether. That's sometimes the way quilts get designed! Don't be daunted by the long cutting instructions – we just wanted to make it very clear. You are doing exactly the same thing all the time but just with different size strips.

Vital Statistics

Quilt Size:	60in x 74in
Block Size:	Variable
Number of Blocks:	Ten each of nine different size flying geese blocks
Setting:	5 vertical rows + 2in centre sashing

Requirements

- Nine fabrics grading from dark (colour 1) to light (colour 9), or for just one fabric you need a total of 2½yd (2.25m)

  Colour 1: ⅛yd (10cm)   Colour 6: ⅜yd (30cm)
  Colour 2: ⅛yd (10cm)   Colour 7: ⅜yd (30cm)
  Colour 3: ⅛yd (10cm)   Colour 8: ⅝yd (50cm)
  Colour 4: ¼yd (20cm)   Colour 9: ⅝yd (60cm)
  Colour 5: ⅜yd (25cm)

- 4yd (3.75m) of background fabric
- ⅝yd (60cm) of binding fabric

Cutting Instructions

COLOUR 1 (DARKEST)

1 Cut one 2½in strip across the width of the fabric. Using the 90 degree triangle and lining up the *2½in strip line* (finished size 2in x 4in) with the bottom of the strip cut ten 90 degree triangles, rotating the ruler 180 degrees as you cut.

 Cut 10 each 2in x 4in

COLOUR 2

2 Cut one 3in strip across the width of the fabric. Using the 90 degree triangle and lining up the *3in strip line* (finished size 2½in x 5in) with the bottom of the strip cut ten 90 degree triangles, rotating the ruler 180 degrees as you cut.

 Cut 10 each 2½in x 5in

COLOUR 3

3 Cut one 3½in strip across the width of the fabric. Using the 90 degree triangle and lining up the *3½in strip line* (finished size 3in x 6in) with the bottom of the strip cut ten 90 degree triangles, rotating the ruler 180 degrees as you cut.

 Cut 10 each 3in x 6in

COLOUR 4

4 Cut two 4in strips across the width of the fabric. Using the 90 degree triangle and lining up the *4in strip line* (finished size 3½in x 7in) with the bottom of the strips cut ten 90 degree triangles, rotating the ruler 180 degrees as you cut.

 Cut 10 each 3½in x 7in

COLOUR 5

5 Cut two 4½in strips across the width of the fabric. Using the 90 degree triangle and lining up the *4½in strip line* (finished size 4in x 8in) with the bottom of the strips cut ten 90 degree triangles, rotating the ruler 180 degrees as you cut.

 Cut 10 each 4in x 8in

COLOUR 6

6 Cut two 5in strips across the width of the fabric. Using the 90 degree triangle and lining up the *5in strip line* (finished 4½in x 9in) with the bottom of the strips cut ten 90 degree triangles, rotating the ruler 180 degree as you cut.

 Cut 10 each 4½in x 9in

COLOUR 7

7 Cut two 5½in strips across the width of the fabric. Using the 90 degree triangle and lining up the *5½in strip line* (finished size 5in x 10in) with the bottom of the strips cut ten 90 degree triangles, rotating the ruler 180 degrees as you cut.

 Cut 10 each 5in x 10in

COLOUR 8

8 Cut three 6in strips across the width of the fabric. Using the 90 degree triangle and lining up the *6in strip line* (finished size 5½in x 11in) with the bottom of the strips cut ten 90 degree triangles, rotating the ruler 180 degrees as you cut.

 Cut 10 each 5½in x 11in

COLOUR 9 (LIGHTEST)

9 Cut three 6½in strips across the width of the fabric. Using the 90 degree triangle and lining up the *6½in strip line* (finished size 6in x 12in) with the bottom of the strips cut ten 90 degree triangles, rotating the ruler 180 degrees as you cut.

 Cut 10 each 6in x 12in

BACKGROUND FABRIC

10 Cut six 2½in strips across the width of the fabric.

- Set two strips aside for the centre sashing strip.
- Using the 45 degree triangle, line up the *2½in strip line* with the bottom of one *folded* strip and cut ten pairs of 2in 45 degree triangles, rotating the ruler 180 degrees as you cut.
- Cut twenty 2½in x 4½in rectangles from three strips.
- Put the triangles and rectangles together in a pile with the 90 degree triangles from the Colour 1 fabric.

 Cut 10 pairs of 2in 45 degree triangles

11 Cut three 3in strips across the width of the fabric.

- Using the 45 degree triangle, line up the *3in strip line* with the bottom of one *folded* strip and cut ten pairs of 2½in 45 degree triangles, rotating the ruler 180 degrees as you cut.
- Cut twenty 3in x 4in rectangles from two strips.
- Put the triangles and rectangles together in a pile with the 90 degree triangles from the Colour 2 fabric.

Cut 10 pairs of 2½in
45 degree triangles

12 Cut three 3½in strips across the width of the fabric.

- Using the 45 degree triangle, line up the *3½in strip line* with the bottom of one *folded* strip and cut ten pairs of 3in 45 degree triangles, rotating the ruler 180 degrees as you cut.
- Cut twenty 3½in squares from two strips.
- Put the triangles and squares together in a pile with the 90 degree triangles from the Colour 3 fabric.

Cut 10 pairs of 3in
45 degree triangles

13 Cut four 4in strips across the width of the fabric.

- Using the 45 degree triangle, line up the *4in strip line* with the bottom of two *folded* strips and cut ten pairs of 3½in 45 degree triangles, rotating the ruler 180 degrees as you cut.
- Cut twenty 3in x 4in rectangles from two strips.
- Put the triangles and rectangles together in a pile with the 90 degree triangles from the Colour 4 fabric.

Cut 10 pairs of 3½in
45 degree triangles

14 Cut four 4½in strips across the width of the fabric.

- Using the 45 degree triangle, line up the *4½in strip line* with the bottom of two *folded* strips and cut ten pairs of 4in 45 degree triangles, rotating the ruler 180 degrees as you cut.
- Cut twenty 2½in x 4½in rectangles from two strips.
- Put the triangles and rectangles together in a pile with the 90 degree triangles from the Colour 5 fabric.

Cut 10 pairs of 4in
45 degree triangles

15 Cut three 5in strips across the width of the fabric.

- Using the 45 degree triangle, line up the *5in strip line* with the bottom of two *folded* strips and cut ten pairs of 4½in 45 degree triangles, rotating the ruler 180 degrees as you cut.
- Cut twenty 2in x 5in rectangles from two strips.
- Put the triangles and rectangles together in a pile with the 90 degree triangles from the Colour 6 fabric.

Cut 10 pairs of 4½in
45 degree triangles

16 Cut three 5½in strips across the width of the fabric.

- Using the 45 degree triangle, line up the *5½in strip line* with the bottom of two *folded* strips and cut ten pairs of 5in 45 degree triangles, rotating the ruler 180 degrees as you cut.
- Cut twenty 1½in x 5½in rectangles from two strips.
- Put the triangles and rectangles together in a pile with the 90 degree triangles from the Colour 7 fabric.

Cut 10 pairs of 5in
45 degree triangles

17 Cut three 6in strips across the width of the fabric.

- Using the 45 degree triangle, line up the *6in strip line* with the bottom of two *folded* strips and cut ten pairs of 5½in 45 degree triangles, rotating the ruler 180 degrees as you cut.
- Cut twenty 1in x 6in rectangles from two strips.
- Put the triangles and rectangles together in a pile with the 90 degrees triangles from the Colour 8 fabric.

Cut 10 pairs of 5½in
45 degree triangles

18 Cut two 6½in strips across the width of the fabric.

- Using the 45 degree triangle, line up the *6½in strip line* with the bottom of two *folded* strips and cut ten pairs of 6in 45 degree triangles, rotating the ruler 180 degree as you cut.
- Put these in a pile with the 90 degree triangles from Colour 9 fabric.

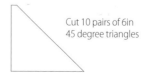

Cut 10 pairs of 6in
45 degree triangles

19 Cut seven 2½in wide strips across the width of the fabric.

Making the Flying Geese Rows

1 Working with the pile of Colour 1 triangles, take one Colour 1 90 degree triangle and sew a 2in background 45 degree triangle cut from a 2½in strip to one side. Press as shown.

2 Sew another 2in background 45 degree triangle to the other side and press.

3 Sew two 2½in x 4½in background rectangles to both sides of this unit and press. Repeat to make ten of these units.

4 Repeat steps 1–3 with the remaining size centre triangles to make ten units from each colourway, making sure you sew the correct size rectangles to each flying geese unit.

5 Sew one unit from each size flying geese together as shown to make one vertical row. Repeat to make ten vertical rows.

6 Sew five vertical rows together as shown, rotating the second and fourth rows 180 degrees to make one half of the quilt. Repeat with the remaining five vertical rows to make an identical second half.

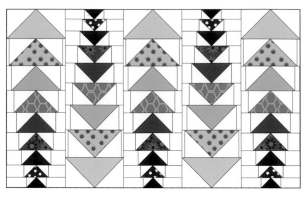

Make 2

Assembling the Quilt

7 Measure the width of these units. Sew two 2½in sashing strips together and then trim to this measurement. Rotate one unit 180 degrees and sew the two units together with the 2½in sashing strip in between. Press the work.

8 Your quilt top is now complete. Quilt and bind as desired.

We used a selection of gorgeous aqua and blue fabrics mostly from the wonderful Tilda collections by Tone Finnengar. However, there are a few other fabrics added to the quilt. Sometimes we get quite particular about using fabrics from the same collection, but don't be, it's good fun to mix them up! Pieced by the authors and longarm quilted by The Quilt Room on a Gammill Statler Stitcher.

Trade Winds

These large quilt blocks are quick to piece and are made from 5in x 10in flying geese units sewn around a centre square. We then made smaller 3in x 6in flying geese units to create the border. Our fabric requirements are given as the total yardage of the colours required but as always we love to use as many fabrics as possible. If you wish your quilt to be as scrappy as ours then cut your strips from a variety of fabrics within the same colourway.

Vital Statistics

Quilt Size:	60in x 75in
Block Size:	15in
Number of Blocks:	12
Setting:	3 x 4 blocks with 1½in inner border and 6in Flying Geese border

Requirements

- 1⅝yd (1.50m) of red fabric
- 1¼yd (1.10m) of green fabric
- 2½yd (2.40m) of background fabric
- ⅝yd (60cm) of binding fabric

Cutting Instructions

RED FABRIC

1 Cut nine 3½in strips across the width of the fabric.

- Using the 45 degree triangle and lining up the *3½in strip line* with the bottom of the *folded* strips, cut nine pairs of 3in 45 degree triangles from each strip, rotating the ruler 180 degrees after each cut. You need seventy-four pairs in total so seven pairs are spare.

Cut 74 pairs of red 3in
45 degree triangles

2 Cut four 5½in strips across the width of the fabric.

- Using the 45 degree triangle and lining up the *5½in strip line* with the bottom of the *folded* strips, cut six pairs of 5in 45 degree triangles from each strip. You need twenty-four pairs in total.

Cut 24 pairs of red 5in
45 degree triangles

GREEN FABRIC

3 Cut six 2in strips across the width of the fabric and set these aside for the inner border.

4 Cut one 6½in strip across the width of the fabric. Subcut into four 6½in squares for the border corners.

5 Cut four 5½in strips across the width of the fabric.

- Using the 45 degree triangle and lining up the *5½in strip line* with the bottom of the *folded* strips, cut six pairs of 5in 45 degree triangles from each strip. You need twenty-four pairs in total.

Cut 24 pairs of green 5in
45 degree triangles

BACKGROUND FABRIC

6 Cut ten 5½in strips across the width of the fabric.

- Take two 5½in strips and subcut each strip into six 5½in squares to make a total of twelve squares for the block centres.
- Using the 90 degree triangle and lining up the *5½in strip line* with the bottom of the strips, cut six 90 degree triangles from each of the remaining eight strips. You need a total of forty-eight.

Cut 48 5in x 10in
90 degree triangles

7 Cut nine 3½in strips across the width of the fabric.

- Using the 90 degree triangle and lining up the *3½in strip line* with the bottom of the strip, cut nine 90 degree triangles from each strip. Repeat with all nine strips to make a total of eighty-one. You need seventy-four so seven are spare.

Cut 74 3in x 6in
90 degree triangles

BINDING FABRIC

8 Cut seven 2½in wide strips across the width of the fabric.

Assembling the Flying Geese Units

1 Sew one 5in green 45 degree triangle to one side of the 5in x 10in background centre triangle as shown and press.

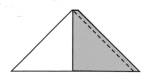

2 Repeat on the other side and press.

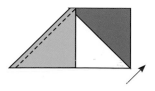

3 Repeat to make twenty-four green 5in x 10in flying geese units.

Make 24

4 Repeat to make twenty-four red 5in x 10in flying geese units.

Make 24

5 Repeat with the 3in red 45 degree triangles and 3in x 6in background 90 degree triangles to make seventy-four 3in x 6in flying geese units for the borders.

Make 74

Assembling the Blocks

6 Take four red 5in x 10in flying geese units and one 5½in background square. With right sides together, partially sew one flying geese unit along the top of the square as shown, starting the seam approximately in the centre of the 5½in square. Carefully press open and this will create a straight edge to sew the next flying geese unit.

Straight edge

Partial seam

7 Sew another 5in x 10in flying geese unit down the right hand side as shown and press open.

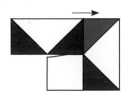

8 Sew another 5in x 10in flying geese unit along the bottom and press open as shown.

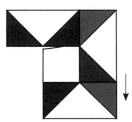

9 Sew the fourth 5in x 10in flying geese unit in place and press open. Complete the partial seam to complete the block and press.

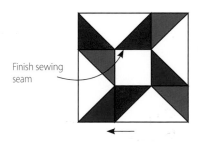

Finish sewing seam

10 Repeat to make a total of six red blocks and six green blocks.

Adding the Borders

11 Join the six 2in wide green strips and sew into a continuous length. Cut two lengths of 60½in which is the vertical measurement of your quilt, and sew these to the sides of your quilt, easing if necessary. Press the seams.

12 Cut two lengths of 48½in, which is the horizontal measurement of your quilt, and sew to the top and bottom, easing if necessary. Your quilt will now measure 48½in x 63½in and this is important to ensure your flying geese border fits nicely.

13 Sew twenty-one 3in x 6in flying geese units together. Repeat to make two of these rows for the side borders of your quilt. Press the seams in one direction.

14 Sew sixteen 3in x 6in flying geese units together as shown and sew a 6½in green square to both ends. Repeat to make two of these rows. Press seams in one direction.

15 Pin and sew the side borders on first, easing if necessary. Make sure the flying geese are pointing in the right direction. Press and then sew on the top and bottom borders, again making sure the flying geese are pointing in the right direction.

16 Your quilt is now complete. Quilt as desired and bind to finish.

The centre of our quilt could have been made using half-square triangles, but we like the idea of using the Flying Geese design throughout. This is especially useful if you are using a large-scale background fabric as it means that you reduce the number of seams. The quilt was made by the authors and longarmed quilted by The Quilt Room.

Jet Stream Jewel

When we were asked to make a quilt to showcase some gorgeous hand-marbled fabric, we jumped at the chance. This is such a simple quilt, which is brought alive by the unique designs created by the hand-marbled fabric. If you want to showcase any fabric you love then this is a quick and easy quilt pattern to follow. A large-scale fabric would also be good to use as the different sections of the fabric will vary in each block.

Vital Statistics

Quilt Size:	38in x 45in
Block Size:	3½ in x 7in
Number of blocks:	40
Setting:	4 vertical rows of 10 blocks, plus 5in border

Requirements:

- ⅝yd (60cm) of showcase fabric
- ⅝yd (60cm) of background fabric
- ⅝yd (60cm) of border fabric (our background and border fabric were the same)
- ½yd (50cm) of binding fabric

Cutting Instructions

SHOWCASE FABRIC

1 Cut five 4in strips across the width of the fabric. Using the 90 degree triangle and lining up the *4in strip line* with the bottom of the strips, cut eight 90 degree triangles from each of the five strips for the centres of the flying geese units. Rotate your ruler 180 degrees after each cut. You need a total of forty.

Cut 40 3½in x 7in 90 degree triangles

BACKGROUND FABRIC

2 Cut five 4in strips across the width of the fabric.

• Using the 45 degree triangle and lining up the *4in strip line* with the bottom of the *folded* strips, cut eights pairs of 3½in 45 degree triangles from each strip. Rotate your ruler 180 degrees after each cut. You need forty pairs in total.

Cut 40 pairs of 3½in 45 degree background triangles

BORDER FABRIC

3 Cut four 5½in strips across the width of the fabric.

BINDING FABRIC

4 Cut five 2½in strips across the width of the fabric.

Assembling the Flying Geese Units

1 Sew one background 45 degree triangle to one side of the flying geese centre triangle, as shown, and then press.

2 Repeat on the other side and press away from the centre triangle.

3 Repeat to make forty 3½in x 7in flying geese units.

Make 40

4 With right sides facing, sew two flying geese units together. Arrange the units so you can see the tip of the triangle over which you are sewing, so your stitching line doesn't cut off the point of the triangle.

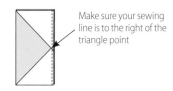

Make sure your sewing line is to the right of the triangle point

5 Sew ten flying geese units together to form one vertical row. Press two with seams pressed down and two with seams pressed up. This will nest the seams together nicely when sewing the rows together.

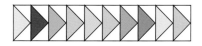

6 Sew the four vertical rows together, pinning at every seam intersection to ensure a perfect match.

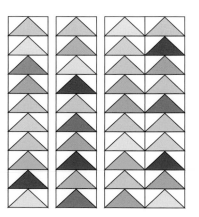

Adding the Border

7 Measure from top to bottom through the centre of the quilt top. Trim two side border strips to this measurement. Stitch the quilt and border together, easing to fit where necessary. Repeat on the opposite side. Press open.

8 Measure from side to side across the centre of the quilt top. Trim two top and bottom border strips to this measurement and sew to the quilt.

9 Your quilt is now complete. Quilt as desired and bind to finish.

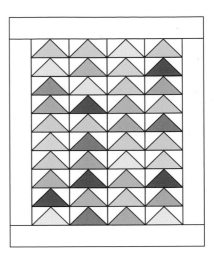

A simple design often works best with fabrics as eye-catching as these. Pam and Nicky made this quilt using hand-marbled fabric from Marbling 4 Fun (see Suppliers). It now hangs proudly on the Marbling 4 Fun stand at all their shows. The quilt was longarmed quilted by The Quilt Room.

Bajan Sunset

Using a combination of three different blocks, all containing flying geese units, half-square triangle units and squares, you can create this complex looking quilt. Be organized and make all your units at the start and then lay them out in separate piles by your sewing machine. Our quilt looks very scrappy but in fact we used only four different half metres. This is one of the benefits of using large-scale prints because when they are cut up into smaller pieces they all look so different. This quilt also shows how to use the flying geese ruler to make half-square triangle units.

Vital Statistics

Quilt Size:	60in x 60in
Block Size:	18in
Number of blocks:	9
Setting:	3 x 3 blocks, plus 3in border

Requirements

- Four ½yd/m of large-scale red/orange fabrics
- 2⅝yd (2.5m) of purple fabric
- ⅝yd (60cm) of binding fabric

Cutting Instructions

RED/ORANGE FABRIC

1 Cut each ½yd into five 3½in wide strips across the width of the fabric to make a total of twenty 3½in strips.

- Take five 3½in strips and using the 90 degree triangle, line up the *3½in strip line* (finished size 3in x 6in) with the bottom of the strip and cut the first triangle. Rotating the ruler along the strip, cut eight 90 degree triangles from each strip. Repeat with all five strips to make a total of forty 3in x 6in 90 degree triangles.

Cut 40 3in x 6in
90 degree triangles

- Take six 3½in strips and using the 45 degree triangle line up the *3½in strip line* on the ruler with the bottom of the *folded* strips and cut eight pairs of 3in 45 degree triangles from each strip, rotating the ruler 180 degrees after each cut. You need forty-eight pairs of 3in 45 degree triangles in total.

Cut 48 pairs of 3in
45 degree triangles

- Take five 3½in strips and cut twelve 3½in squares from each strip to make a total of sixty.

Cut 60 3½in squares

- Leave four 3½in strips uncut to make the red and purple half-square triangle units.

PURPLE FABRIC

2 Cut one 6½in strip across the width of the fabric and subcut into five 6½in squares.

- Cut twenty-three 3½in strips across the width of the fabric.

    - Take six 3½in strips and using the 90 degree triangle, line up the *3½in strip line* (finished size 3in x 6in) with the bottom of the strip and cut the first triangle. Rotating the ruler along the strip, cut eight 90 degree triangles from each strip. Repeat with all six strips to make a total of forty-eight 3in x 6in triangles.

Cut 48 3in x 6in
90 degree triangles

    - Take five 3½in strips and using the 45 degree triangle line up the *3½in strip line* on the ruler with the bottom of the *folded* strips and cut eight pairs of triangles from each strip, rotating the ruler 180 degrees after each cut. You need forty pairs of 3in 45 degree triangles in total.

Cut 40 pairs of 3in
45 degree triangles

    - Take eight 3½in strips and cut one 3½in x 24½in rectangle and two 3½in squares from each strip to make a total of eight 3½in x 24½in rectangles and sixteen 3½in squares. The balance of these strips is spare.

Cut 16
3½in squares   Cut 8 3½in x 24½in rectangles

- Leave four 3½in strips uncut to make the red and purple half-square triangle units.

BINDING FABRIC

3 Cut seven 2½in wide strips across the width of the fabric

Making the Flying Geese Units

1 Sew a purple 45 degree triangle to one side of a red 90 degree triangle, and then press open as shown. Repeat on the other side and press open to form flying geese Unit A. Repeat to make forty Unit A.

Make 40 flying geese
– Unit A

2 Sew one red 3in 45 degree triangle to one side of a purple 90 degree triangle and press open as shown.

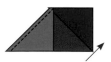

3 Repeat on the other side and press open to form flying geese Unit B. Repeat to make forty-eight Unit B.

Make 48 flying geese
– Unit B

Making the Half-Square Triangle Units

4 Take a 3½in red strip and a 3½in purple strip and press right sides together ensuring that they are exactly one on top of the other. The pressing will help hold the two strips together.

5 Lay them out on a cutting mat and position the 45 degree triangle as shown, lining up the *3½in strip line* with the bottom edge of the strips. Trim the selvedge and cut the first triangle. Rotate the ruler 180 degrees and cut the next triangle. Continue along the strip to cut sixteen pairs of triangles from each strip.

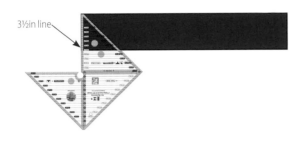

3½in line

6 Sew along the diagonal of each pair of triangles. Trim the dog ears and press open towards the dark fabric to form sixteen half-square triangle units. Repeat with all four red strips and four purple strips allocated for the half-square triangle units. You need sixty-four half-square triangle units in total.

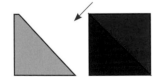

Make 64 half-square triangle units

Making the Rising Star Blocks

7 You need to make four Rising Star blocks. Choose the following for each of the four blocks.

- Eight flying geese Unit A.
- Eight half-square triangle units.
- Eight red/orange 3½in squares.
- One purple 6½in square.

8 To piece the block, sew the flying geese Unit As together and press as shown. Now sew the corner units together and press as shown, pinning at every seam intersection to ensure a perfect match.

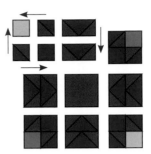

9 Sew the units into rows and sew the rows together, pressing rows in alternate directions wherever possible so the seams nest together nicely. Repeat this process to make four Rising Star blocks.

Making Cup and Saucer Blocks

10 You need to make four Cup and Saucer blocks. Choose the following for each of the four blocks.

- Ten flying geese Unit B.
- Eight half-square triangle units.
- Four red/orange 3½in squares.
- Four purple 3½in squares.

11 To piece the block sew the flying geese Unit Bs together and press as shown. Now sew the corner units together pinning at every seam intersection to ensure a perfect match. Press as shown.

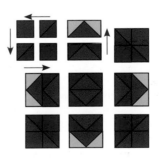

12 Sew the units into rows and then sew the rows together, pressing rows in alternate directions wherever possible so the seams nest together nicely. Repeat this process to make four Cup and Saucer blocks.

Making the Eddystone Light Block

13 You need to make one Eddystone Light block. Choose the following for the block.

- Four flying geese Unit A.
- Eight flying geese Unit B.
- Eight red/orange 3½in squares.
- One purple 6½in square

14 Tp piece the block sew a flying geese Unit A to both sides of the 6½in purple square as shown and press towards the centre.

15 Sew a 3½in red square to both sides of two flying geese Unit As, pressing to the squares. Sew this unit to the top and bottom of the centre unit.

16 Sew the outer flying geese Unit Bs as shown and sew to both sides of the centre unit.

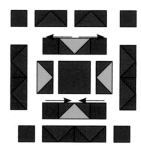

17 Join the top and bottom rows and sew to the top and bottom of the centre unit, pinning at every seam intersection for a perfect match.

Assembling the Quilt

18 Lay out the nine blocks with the Eddystone Light block in the centre and the Rising Star blocks in the four corners. When you are happy with the arrangement, sew the blocks into rows, pinning at every seam intersection to ensure a perfect match. Press rows 1 and 3 to the left and row 2 to the right, so the seams will nest together nicely when sewing the rows together.

19 Now sew the rows together, pinning at every seam intersection. Press the seams.

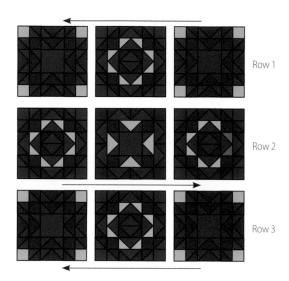

Row 1

Row 2

Row 3

Adding the Border

20 Sew two 3½in x 24½in rectangles to both sides of one flying geese Unit A. Repeat to make two side inner borders.

21 Sew two 3½in x 24½in rectangles to both sides of one flying geese Unit A and sew a red 3½in square to both ends. Repeat to make two for the top and bottom borders.

Side border - make 2

Top and bottom border - make 2

22 Pin and sew the side borders on first, easing where necessary, and then press. Sew the top and bottom borders on and then press.

23 Your quilt top is now complete. Quilt as desired and bind to finish.

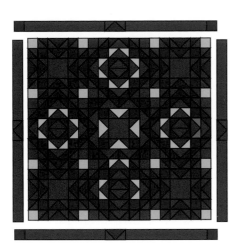

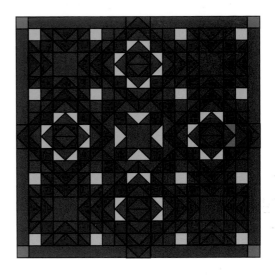

This quilt uses fabrics by Kaffe Fassett. We love his large-scale prints, which when cut into small pieces take on a whole new look. We decided on a purple coordinating fabric to enrich the quilt and make the blocks come alive. Pieced by the authors and longarm quilted by The Quilt Room on a Gammill Statler Stitcher.

Coastal Paths

We have given yardage requirements for this quilt but if you have some spare jelly roll strips this is the perfect quilt to use them up as we used just sixteen 2½in wide strips and background fabric. We love the scrappy effect the jelly roll strips create in this quilt so if you do have some spare strips this is how to sort them. We used three different strips each of pink, blue, green and yellow, two different strips of grey plus one strip each of blue and green for sashing squares. Just add four yards of background fabric, mix well and hey presto – you have one beautiful quilt.

Vital Statistics

Quilt Size:	61¼in x 61¼in
Block Size:	17¾in
Number of blocks:	9
Setting:	3 x 3 blocks, plus 2in border

Requirements

- Long ¼yd/m of blue, green, yellow and pink fabrics
- Long ¼yd/m of grey fabric
- Long ¼yd/m of fabric for sashing squares
- 4yd (3.6m) of background fabric
- ⅝yd (60cm) of binding fabric

Cutting Instructions

BLUE, GREEN, YELLOW AND PINK FABRIC

1 Cut each fabric into three 2½in wide strips across the width of the fabric to make a total of twelve strips.

- Take each of the strips and using the 90 degree triangle, line up the *2½in strip line* (finished size 2in x 4in) with the bottom of the strip. Cut twelve 90 degree triangles from each strip to make a total of 144 2in x 4in 90 degree triangles for the flying geese centres, rotating your ruler 180 degrees as you cut. You will have thirty-six in each of the four colours.

Cut 144 2in x 4in
90 degree triangles

GREY FABRIC

2 Cut two 2½in wide strips across the width of the fabric. Using the 90 degree triangle, line up the *2½in strip line* (finished size 2in x 4in) with the bottom of the strips and cut a total of eighteen 2in x 4in 90 degree triangles for the flying geese centre triangles, rotating your ruler 180 degrees as you cut.

Cut 18 grey 2in x 4in
90 degree triangles

SASHING SQUARES

3 Cut two 2½in wide strips across the width of the fabric and subcut into a total of sixteen 2½in squares.

BACKGROUND FABRIC

4 Cut twenty-six 2½in strips across the width of the fabric.

- Take twelve 2½in strips and cut each strip into two 2½in x 18¼in rectangles to make a total of twenty-four sashing strips.
- Take fourteen 2½in strips and using the 45 degree triangle, line up the *2½in strip line* with the bottom of the *folded* strips and cut twelve pairs of 2in 45 degree triangles from each strip, rotating your ruler 180 degrees as you cut. You need 162 pairs in total so six pairs are spare.

Cut 162 pairs of
2in background
45 degree triangles

- Cut nine 6½in strips across the width of the fabric and using the 90° triangle line up the *6½in strip line* with the bottom of the strip and cut each strip into four 90 degree triangles to make a total of thirty-six setting triangles, rotating your ruler 180 degrees as you cut.

Cut 36
6in setting triangles

- Cut three 4in strips across the width of the fabrics. Using the 45 degree triangle, line up the *4in strip line* with the bottom of the strips and cut a total of thirty-six 45 degree triangles for the corners of the blocks, rotating your ruler 180 degrees as you cut.

Cut 36
corner triangles

BORDER FABRIC

5 Cut six 2½in strips across the width of the fabric.

BINDING FABRIC

6 Cut seven 2½in strips across the width of the fabric

Assembling the Flying Geese Units

1 Sew one background 45 degree triangle to one side of a 90 degree flying geese centre triangle, as shown and press.

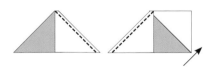

2 Repeat on the other side and press the flying geese unit.

3 Repeat to make thirty-six each of blue, green, pink and yellow flying geese units and eighteen grey flying geese units. Chain piecing will speed up this process.

Make 36 of each

Make 18

Assembling the Blocks

4 Take two grey flying geese units and, pinning at all of the seam intersections, sew together as shown to make a centre square. Repeat to make nine centre squares.

Make 9
centre squares

5 Take one each of the blue, green, pink and yellow units, sew them together as shown to make Unit A and press. Repeat to make thirty-six Unit A.

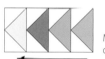

Make 36
of Unit A

6 Sew two Unit As together, with a centre square in the middle to make the centre row of the block. Repeat to make nine centre rows.

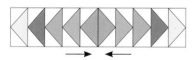

Make 9
centre rows

7 Sew a setting triangle to both sides of a Unit A and press as shown. Repeat to make eighteen of these units. The setting triangles are cut slightly larger so when sewing the setting triangles make sure the bottom of the triangle is aligned with the bottom of the block.

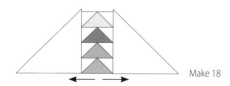

Make 18

8 Take two of these units and sew them together with a centre row in between. Pin at every seam intersection to ensure a perfect match. Repeat to make nine blocks.

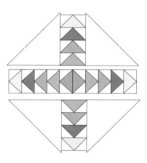

9 Sew on the corner triangles and trim to square up the blocks. The blocks should each measure 18¼in square.

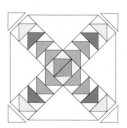

Assembling the Quilt

10 Sew four 2½in x 18¼in sashing strips together with three blocks to make one row, as shown, and press as shown. Repeat to make three rows in total.

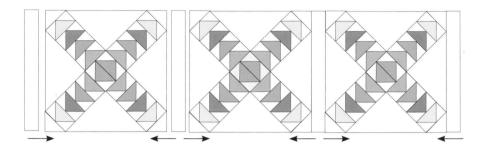

11 Sew three 2½in x 18¼in sashing strips together with four 2½in sashing squares. Press towards the sashing squares. Repeat to make four sashing strip rows.

12 Sew the three rows together with the four sashing strip rows as shown, pinning at every seam intersection to ensure a perfect match. Press the work.

13 Your quilt top is now complete. Quilt as desired and bind to finish.

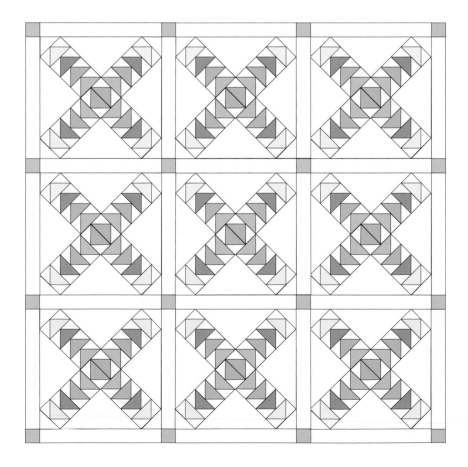

You can really see the longarm quilting in this quilt. We used a lovely dancing hearts pattern coupled with a neutral thread to let the pattern 'sink' into the quilts. We used a range of pastel colours but you could use a selection from just one colourway combined with background fabric. Pieced by the authors and longarm quilted by The Quilt Room on a Gammill Statler Stitcher.

Geometric Breeze

Making flying geese units is such fun and using a ruler created specially for making them makes life so much easier. Speciality rulers, however, are sometimes even more clever than we think. Certainly the Creative Grids Multi-Size Flying Geese & 45°/90° Triangle can do lots more and we just wanted to give you a taster of what else it can do. Strip tube cutting is a fun technique that creates a variety of effects and in this quilt we describe the technique and show you how to make two different blocks, which can be combined to make a stunning quilt.

Vital Statistics

Quilt size: 55in x 55in
Block size: 8½in
Number of blocks: 36
Setting: 6 x 6 blocks, plus 2in wide border

Requirements

- 1yd (90cm) of blue fabric
- 1yd (90cm) of red fabric
- 1yd (90cm) of green fabric
- 1⅛yd (1.10m) of background and border fabric
- ½yd (50cm) of binding fabric

TIP A jelly roll could be used to make a scrappier quilt but it would need to be divided into three colourways to provide twelve strips in each colourway.

Cutting Instructions

BLUE, RED AND GREEN FABRIC

1 Cut each fabric colour into twelve 2½in wide strips across the width of the fabric.

BACKGROUND AND BORDER FABRIC

2 Cut four 6½in wide strips across the width of the fabric.

· Cut five 2½in wide strips across the width of the fabric and set aside for the borders.

BINDING FABRIC

3 Cut six 2½in wide strips across the width of the fabric.

Making the Blocks

1 Take one strip from each colourway and sew together down the long sides. Press the seams in one direction. Repeat to make twelve of these strip units always *keeping the colours in the same order*.

Make 12

2 Take two of the strip units and place them right sides together, rotating one strip unit 180 degrees. Make sure the seams nest up against each other all the way along the strip unit – pin in place to stop any movement. Sew a scant ¼in seam along both sides of the strip unit to form a tube. Repeat to make four tubes.

Make 4

3 Lay the 90 degree triangle on the tube as shown, lining up the 6½in strip line along the bottom of the strip units. Cut either side of triangle.

6½in strip line

4 Rotate the triangle along the tube to cut five triangles.

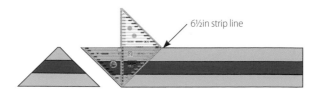

6½in strip line

5 Gently pick up each triangle and unpick the few threads that are along the tip of the triangle. You are dealing with bias edges now so care must be taken not to pull the fabric too much.

Carefully unpick these threads

6 Gently press open, pressing the seams towards the blue fabric. Make a total of twenty of these blocks.

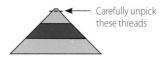

Make 20

7 Using the remaining four strip units and the four 6½in wide background strips, place right sides together and sew a scant ¼in seam along both sides of the strip unit to form a tube. Repeat to make four tubes in total.

8 Using the 90 degree triangle as shown in steps 3 and 4, cut four triangles from each strip unit to make a total of sixteen triangles. Gently press open and press seams towards the background fabric. You will have eight each of two types of blocks, as shown.

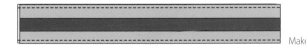

Make 4

Make 8

Make 8

Assembling the Quilt

9 Referring to the diagram, arrange the blocks as shown, double checking that you have positioned them correctly. When you are happy with the arrangement sew the blocks into rows and then sew the rows together. Press the seams of alternate rows in opposite directions, so that the seams nest together nicely when sewing the rows together.

Adding the Border

10 Join the border strips into a continuous length. Determine the vertical measurement from top to bottom through the centre of your quilt top. Cut two side borders to this measurement.

11 Mark the halves and quarters of one quilt side and one border with pins. Placing right sides together and matching the pins, stitch the quilt and border together, easing the quilt side to fit where necessary. Repeat on the opposite side. Press the seams.

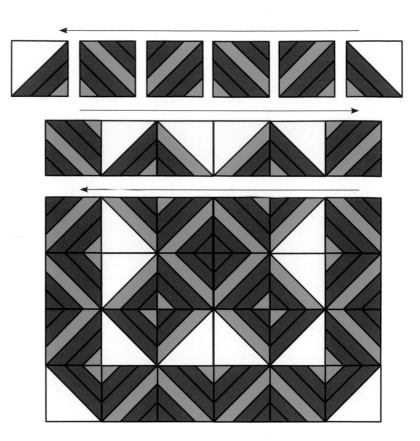

12 Now determine the horizontal measurement from side to side across the centre of the quilt top. Cut two borders to this measurement. Pin and sew to the top and bottom of your quilt and press.

13 Your quilt is now complete. Quilt as desired and bind to finish.

We love the bright and striking contrast our fabrics give us and this contrast really helps show off the geometric design. This is such a quick technique and one we have used time and time again as it produces such striking results! Pieced by the authors and longarm quilted by The Quilt Room on a Gammill Statler Stitcher.

General Techniques

Pressing

In quilt making, pressing is of vital importance and if extra care is taken you will be well rewarded. This is especially true when dealing with strips. If your strips start bowing and stretching you will lose accuracy.

- Always set your seam after sewing by pressing the seam as sewn, without opening up your strips. This eases any tension and prevents the seam line from distorting. Move the iron with an up and down motion, zigzagging along the seam rather than ironing down the length of the seam, which could cause distortion.
- Open up your strips and press on the *right* side, towards the darker fabric, if necessary guiding the seam underneath to make sure it is going in the right direction. Press with an up and down motion rather than along the length of the strip.
- Always take care if using steam and certainly don't use steam anywhere near a bias edge.
- When you are joining more than two strips together, press the seams after attaching each strip. You are more likely to get bowing if you leave it until your strip unit is complete before pressing.
- Each seam must be pressed flat before another seam is sewn across it. Unless there is a special reason for not doing so, seams are pressed towards the darker fabric. The main criteria when joining seams is to have seam allowances going in the opposite direction to each other as they then nest together without bulk. Your patchwork will lie flat and your seam intersections will be accurate.

Pinning

When you have to align a seam it is important to insert pins to stop any movement when sewing. Long, fine pins with flat heads are recommended as they will go through the layers of fabric easily and allow you to sew up to and over them.

Seams should always be pressed in opposite directions so they will nest together nicely. Insert a pin either at right angles or diagonally through the seam intersection ensuring that the seams are matching perfectly. When sewing, do not remove the pin too early as your fabric might shift and your seams will not be perfectly aligned.

Chain Piecing

Chain piecing is the technique of feeding a series of pieces through the sewing machine without lifting the presser foot and without cutting the thread between each piece, which saves time and thread. Once your chain is complete, snip the thread between the pieces.

When chain piecing shapes other than squares and rectangles it is sometimes preferable when finishing one shape, to lift the presser foot slightly and reposition on the next shape, still leaving the thread uncut.

Removing Dog Ears

A dog ear is the excess piece of fabric that overlaps past the seam allowance when sewing triangles to other shapes. Dog ears should always be cut off to reduce bulk. They can be trimmed using a rotary cutter or snipped with small scissors. Make sure you are trimming the points parallel to the straight edge of the triangle.

Joining Border and Binding Strips

If you need to join strips for your borders and binding, you may choose to join them with a diagonal seam to make them less noticeable. Press the seams open.

Adding Borders

The fabric requirements in this book all assume you are going to be sewing straight rather than mitred borders. If you intend to have mitred borders please add sufficient extra fabric for this.

Adding straight borders

1 Determine the vertical measurement from top to bottom through the centre of your quilt top. Cut two side border strips to this measurement. Mark the halves and quarters of one quilt side and one border with pins. Placing right sides together and matching the pins, stitch the quilt and border together, easing the quilt side to fit where necessary. Repeat on the opposite side. Press open.

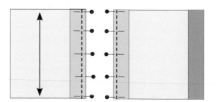

2 Determine the horizontal measurement from side to side across the centre of the quilt top. Cut two top and bottom border strips to this measurement and add to the quilt top in the same manner.

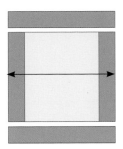

Quilting

Quilting stitches hold the patchwork top, wadding (batting) and backing together and create texture over your finished patchwork. The choice is yours whether you hand quilt, machine quilt or send it off to a longarm quilting service. There are many books on the techniques of hand and machine quilting but the basic procedure is as follows.

1 With the aid of templates or a ruler, mark out the quilting lines on the patchwork top.

2 Cut the backing fabric and wadding at least 4in larger all around than the patchwork top. Pin or tack (baste) the layers together to prepare them for quilting.

3 Quilt either by hand or by machine. Remove any quilting marks on completion of the quilting.

Binding a Quilt

The fabric requirements in this book are for a 2½in double-fold binding cut on the straight grain.

1 Trim the excess backing and wadding (batting) so that the edges are even with the top of the quilt. Join your binding strips into a continuous length, making sure there is sufficient to go around the quilt plus 8in–10in for corners and overlapping ends. With wrong sides together, press the binding in half lengthways. Fold and press under ½in to neaten the edge at the end where you will start sewing.

2 On the right side of the quilt and starting about 12in away from a corner, align the edges of the double thickness binding with the edge of the quilt so that the cut edges are towards the edges of the quilt and pin to hold in place. Sew with a ¼in seam allowance, leaving the first inch open.

3 At the first corner, stop ¼in from the edge of the fabric and

backstitch. Lift the needle and presser foot and fold the binding upwards (see diagram). Fold the binding again but downwards. Stitch from the edge to ¼in from the next corner and repeat the turn. Continue all around the quilt working each corner in the same way. When you come to the starting point, cut the binding, fold under the cut edge and overlap at the starting point.

4 Fold the binding over to the back of the quilt and hand stitch in place, folding the binding at each corner to form a neat mitre.

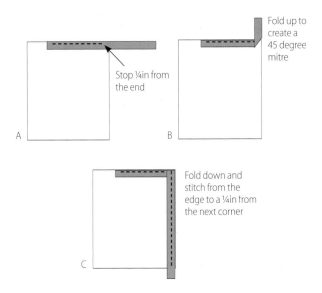

Stop ¼in from the end

A

B

Fold up to create a 45 degree mitre

C

Fold down and stitch from the edge to a ¼in from the next corner

Making a Larger Quilt

If you want to make a larger version of any of the quilts in the book, refer to the Vital Statistics of the quilt, which shows the block size, the number of blocks, how the blocks are set, plus the size of border used. You can then calculate your requirements for a larger quilt.

Setting on Point

Any block can take on a totally new look when set on point and you might like to try one of the quilts to see what it looks like on point. For this reason we have included information for setting quilts on point. Some people are a little daunted as there are a few things to take into consideration but here is all you need to know.

How wide will my blocks be when set on point?

To calculate the measurement of the block from point to point you multiply the size of the finished block by 1.414. Example: a 12in block will measure 12in x 1.414 which is 16.97in – just under 17in. Now you can calculate how many blocks you need for your quilt.

How do I piece blocks on point?

Piece rows diagonally, starting at a corner. Triangles have to be added to the end of each row before joining the rows and these are called setting triangles.

What size setting triangles do I cut?

Setting triangles form the outside of your quilt and need to have the straight of grain on the outside edge to prevent stretching. To ensure this, these triangles are formed from quarter-square triangles, i.e., a square cut into four. The measurement for this is: Diagonal Block Size + 1¼in. Example: a 12in block (diagonal measurement approximately 17in) should be 18¼in.

Corners triangles are added last. They also need to have the outside edge on the straight of grain so these should be cut from half-square triangles. To calculate the size of square to cut in half, divide the finished size of your block by 1.414 then add ⅞in. Example: a 12in block would be 12in divided by 1.414 = 8.49in + ⅞in (0.88) = 9.37in (or 9½in as it can be trimmed later).

Most diagonal quilts start off with one block and in each row thereafter the number of blocks increases by two. All rows contain an odd number of blocks. To calculate the quilt's finished size, count the number of diagonals across and multiply this by the diagonal measurement of the block. Do the same with the number of blocks down and multiply this by the diagonal measurement of the block.

If you want a rectangular quilt instead of a square one, count the number of blocks in the row that establishes the width and repeat that number in following rows until the desired length is established.

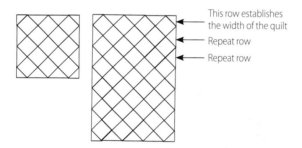

This row establishes the width of the quilt
← Repeat row
← Repeat row

Calculating Backing Fabric

There are various widths of backing fabrics now available. Bear in mind that whichever width you choose that your backing fabric should be 3in–4in larger than your quilt top on all sides. We have given yardage here for the quilts in this book for 42in wide and 108in wide.

	42in wide fabric	108in wide fabric
Flower Power	3¼yd	1⅝yd
Roman Holiday	4¼yd	2¼yd
Stargazing	4¼yd	2¼yd
Starry Skies	4¼yd	2¼yd
Scattered Squares	3½yd	1¾yd
Circular Motion	3½yd	1¾yd
Friday Night	1¼yd	not suitable
Saturday Morning	3¼yd	1¾yd
Misty Mountain	3½yd	1¾yd
Two to Tango	3yd	1½yd
Jubilee	3⅝yd	2yd
Playtime	3¼yd	1⅝yd
Flight to Paradise	3¾yd	1⅞yd
Trade Winds	3¾yd	1⅞yd
Jet Stream Jewel	1½yd	not suitable
Bajan Sunset	3¾yd	1⅞yd
Coastal Paths	3¾yd	1⅞yd
Geometric Breeze	3yd	1½yd

Using 60in wide fabric

This is a simple calculation as to how much you need to buy. Example: your quilt is 54in x 72in. Your backing needs to be 3in larger all round so your backing measurement is 60in x 78in. If you have found 60in wide backing, then you would buy the length which is 78in. However, if you have found 90in wide backing, you can turn it round and you would only have to buy the width of 60in.

Using 42in wide fabric

You will need to have a join or joins in order to get the required measurement unless the backing measurement for your quilt is 42in or less on one side. If your backing measurement is less than 42in then you need only buy one length.

Using the previous example, if your backing measurement is 60in x 78in, you will have to have one seam somewhere in your backing. If you join two lengths of 42in fabric together your new fabric measurement will be 84in (less a little for the seam). This would be sufficient for the length of your quilt so you need to buy twice the width, i.e., 60in x 2 = 120in. Your seam will run horizontal.

If your quilt length is more than your new backing fabric measurement of 84in you will need to use the measurement of 84in for the width of your quilt and you will have to buy twice the length. Your seam will then run vertical.

Templates

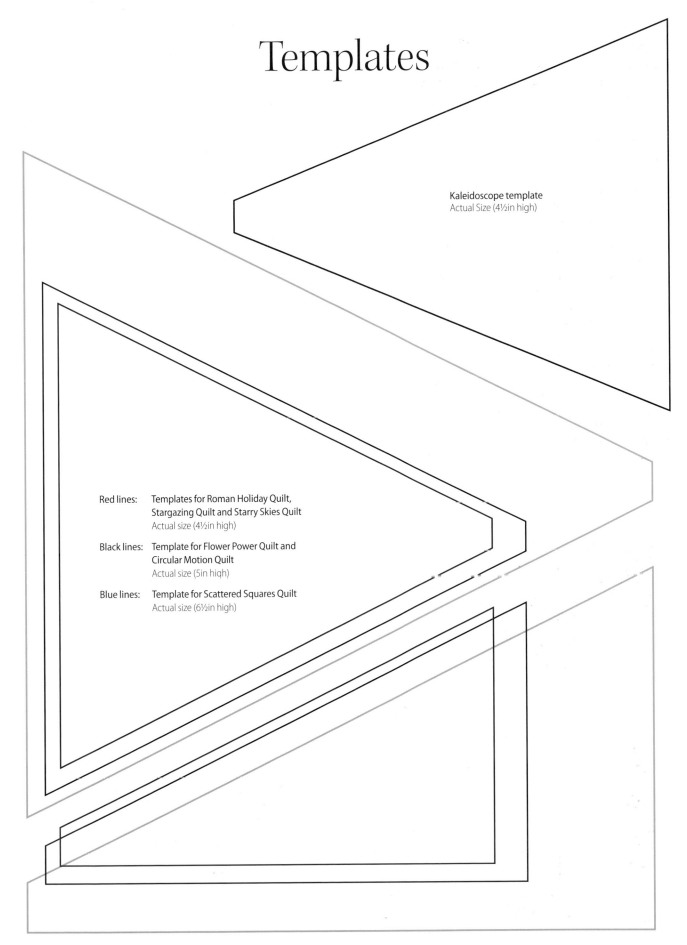

Kaleidoscope template
Actual Size (4½in high)

Red lines: Templates for Roman Holiday Quilt,
              Stargazing Quilt and Starry Skies Quilt
              Actual size (4½in high)

Black lines: Template for Flower Power Quilt and
              Circular Motion Quilt
              Actual size (5in hiqh)

Blue lines: Template for Scattered Squares Quilt
              Actual size (6½in high)

About the Authors

Pam Lintott opened her shop, The Quilt Room, in 1981, which she still runs today, along with her daughter Nicky. Pam is the author of *The Quilt Room Patchwork & Quilting Workshops*, as well as *The Quilter's Workbook*. The shop, together with the mail order department and longarm quilting department, are housed in a 15th century inn located in the historic market town of Dorking, Surrey just south of London, UK. *Quick Quilts With Rulers* is Pam and Nicky's tenth book for David & Charles following on from their eight extremely popular Jelly Roll Quilt books, including the phenomenally successful *Jelly Roll Quilts*.

Acknowledgments

First of all, Pam and Nicky would like to thank Rachel and Mathew Cross of Creative Grids UK for designing such great rulers and for their encouragement and support in the production of this book. They would also like to thank The Quilt Room team and the efficient quilters from Cornwall who are always willing to test the patterns. Their thanks and gratitude go to Gammill for providing such an amazing longarm quilting machine to enable them to quilt all the projects in the shortest possible time, and to Janome UK for allowing the use of their reliable sewing machines. Last, but not least, hugs and kisses to their husbands Nick and Rob for continuing to look after domestic chores when computers and sewing machines are working overtime!

Suppliers

THE QUILT ROOM
(Shop, Mail Order and Gammill UK Dealers)
37–39 High Street, Dorking,
Surrey RH4 1AR, UK
Tel: 01306 877307
www.quiltroom.co.uk

CREATIVE GRIDS (UK) LTD
23A Pate Road, Melton Mowbray,
Leicestershire LE13 0RG, UK
Tel: 01455 828667
www.creativegrids.com

GAMMILL INC
1452 W. Gibson, West Plains, MO. 65775, USA
www.gammill.net

JANOME UK LTD
Janome Centre, Southside,
Stockport, Cheshire SK6 2SP, UK
Tel: 0161 666 6011
www.janome.com

MARBLING 4 FUN
Email: marbling4fun@gmail.com
www.marbling4fun.net

STITCH CRAFT CREATE
Brunel House, Forde Close, Newton Abbot,
Devon, TQ12 4PU, UK
Tel: 0844 8805852
www.stitchcraftcreate.co.uk

MARTHA PULLEN
149 Old Big Cove Road,
Brownsboro, AL 35741, USA
www.marthapullen.com

Index

A DAVID & CHARLES BOOK

© F&W Media International, Ltd, 2014

Originally published in the UK in 2012/13 by
Lynher Publications as 3 booklets:

*Three Patterns Featuring Creative Grids®
Double-strip Kaleidoscope Ruler*

*Three Patterns Featuring Creative Grids®
Multi-Size 2 Peaks in 1 Triangle Ruler*

Flying Geese Multi-Size

David & Charles is an imprint of F&W Media International, Ltd
Brunel House, Forde Close, Newton Abbot, TQ12 4PU, UK

F&W Media International, Ltd is a subsidiary of F+W Media, Inc
10151 Carver Road, Suite #200, Blue Ash, OH 45242, USA

Text and Designs © Pam & Nicky Lintott, Rachel and Matthew Cross
2013 except Flying Geese chapter which is © Pam & Nicky Lintott
Layout © F&W Media International, Ltd 2013

Photography © Pam & Nicky Lintott 2012, except those
on pages 2, 6, 27, 31, 33, 36, 37, 39, 40, 44, 45, 46, 57, 58,
59, 63, 65, 67, 69, 71, 93, 97, 99, 109, 113, 115, 118 and 121
which are © F&W Media International, Ltd 2013

A catalogue record for this book is available from the British Library.

ISBN-13: 978-1-4463-0469-3 paperback/hardback
ISBN-10: 1-4463-0469-8 paperback/hardback

Printed in China by RR Donnelley for:
F&W Media International, Ltd
Brunel House, Forde Close, Newton Abbot, TQ12 4PU, UK

10 9 8 7 6 5 4 3 2 1

Acquisitions Editor: Sarah Callard
Desk Editor: Matthew Hutchings
Project Editor: Linda Clements
Designer: Jennifer Stanley
Photographer: Jack Kirby and Jack Gorman
Production Controller: Kelly Smith

F+W Media publishes high quality books on a wide range of subjects.
For more great book ideas visit: www.stitchcraftcreate.co.uk